# Just be Real

## What Kind of Image Are You Exposing? ●

BY

# Elder Charlie A. Connor III

Tate Publishing, LLC

To Make Sure You Know And Believe The
Devil Is A Liar, You Must Not Live A Lie!!!

Connor Ministries
Richmond Virginia

# Preface

When hearing the words "Just be real," we automatically think this means telling someone how it really is, and to speak what is on our mind. Don't talk behind people's back, but speak to their face. Simply be real or be still. Yet we miss the real reason we need to be real. We are told to be real with people and situations and forget about "just being real" with God—the one who really matters.

Many times we, as believers, face this problem, and we don't even realize it. When we are not real with ourselves, it is impossible to be real with God. It is very easy to be real as people pleasers, and God isn't even in the picture. Therefore, all of our realness is in vain. But when we lean and depend on God, he will teach us how to be real.

This book will teach and show you principles of real life experiences by simply showing you the real you. This book is based upon the best teacher "experience" and the word of God. The word is implemented and broken down chapter to chapter. While reading, your spirit will receive Bible based principles and reasons to "just be real" with yourself. Then you can be real with God. You will be shocked when you realize how much you are being real with your walk with God, as well as with yourself. Once you are real with yourself and real with God, you can be real to others and see life with a real eye as you are led by the Holy Spirit.

"Just Be Real" is the first of many books from me that will encourage, uplift, and deliver many people by just reading, accepting, and then living according to the word of God. Be Blessed as you read "Just Be Real."

Elder Charlie A. Connor III

# Foreword

"Search me, O God, and Know my heart; Try me, and know my thoughts; and see if there is any wicked way in me, and lead me in the way everlasting" (Psalm 139:23,24).

This scripture relates directly to "Just Be Real". As we embark upon our walk with Christ, we have to continuously ask the Lord to search our hearts so we can "Just Be Real" in our Christian walk. I've known the author all of his life, and watched as he began to truly walk in his calling as his ministry began to blossom. Taking the word from North Carolina to Virginia and wherever he is called upon to go, Charlie A. Connor III is letting his light shine. Now, God has inspired him to write "Just Be Real" to encourage Christians today to let God show us who we are. As part of his ministry, "Just Be Real" is just the foundation in all the things that the Lord is going to do through him. This book, though short in length, has a powerful message for God's people. As the scripture says, "Cry loud and spare not." Charlie is doing just that in "Just Be Real". Reading this book will help us see ourselves, and just how fair our hearts truly are from the Lord. This book should be shared with all those truly seeking to develop an intimate relationship with our Lord and Savior. As you read this book, know that the man of God who penned it is truly on the battlefield for the Lord. He's trying to encourage God's people to come up to their rightful place in order to fulfill the destiny that God is calling them to. Allow God to bless you in the reading of "Just Be Real".

Evangelist Cortina Dixon
Washington Chapel Church Kinston, North Carolina

# Ackowledgements

These words will never show my true appreciation to all those that played a part in my spiritual and personal life and inspired me to write this book. My appreciation and sincere thanks go out to you all, and even to those that buy and read my first book.

I give praise and thanks to my Lord and Savior Jesus Christ. Without him, none of this would be possible.

Thanks to my beautiful, wonderful, supporting, gracious, and understanding wife and best friend, Michelle R. Connor. Without her love and support, I would not be where I am today. Thank God for my son Terrance E. Connor, who is my biggest fan and my greatest accomplishment in life.

Thank God for my mother, Ellen J. Connor, and late father, Charlie A. Connor II, for their unconditional love and support. They shaped me into the man I am today by always believing in me and encouraging me to make my dreams come true. Thank God for my brother, William E. Jones, for always taking up for me in my time of trouble and coming to my defense when no one else would. Thank God for my older sister, Cortina C. Dixon, for her spiritual support and wisdom to help me stay focused on the things of God. Thank God for my younger sister, Megan E. Connor, for trusting me enough to take my God given advice and allow it to help her in her times of struggle. It made her the great woman of God she is today.

Thank God for Pastor Timothy and First Lady Bridgette Jones from Washington Chapel Church in Kinston, NC, and the entire church family for their prayers and support during this publishing process. Thank God for Evangelist Debbie Brown for her spiritual guidance during my walk with God.

Thank God for my pastors here in Virginia, Pastor Sherman and Sharon Spratley from Victory and Praise Family Worship Ministries in Hopewell, VA. Truly a family that prays together stays together. Thanks to the entire church family of Victory and Praise Family Worship Ministries.

Thank God for my true friends: Marvin L. Connor, Annie Connor, Gloshonda Flemings, Tyron Flemings, Robert Young Jr., Gerry Wootson, and Angela Lewis. Their support through the tough times in my life helped me stay on target with God.

Thank God for my grandparents, Queenester Connor and Winnie Jones, for their advice, guidance, and support as I embarked on this Christian journey. Thank God for all of my aunts, uncles, cousins, friends, co-workers, and saints for their support and encouraging words.

Thank God for Tate Publishing Company and all those that played a part in making my dream come true as I encourage others to "Just Be Real."


Sincerely,

Elder Charlie A. Connor III

# Table of Content

# Chapter 1

## Being Introduced To God:

That if thou shalt confess with thou mouth the Lord Jesus And shalt believe in thine heart that God hath raised Him from the dead,. thou shalt be saved (Romans 10:9).

I remember as far back as being seven years old when I first experienced being in a church. I remember sitting through Sunday school with my aunt and my two cousins as we awaited others to arrive. While we were waiting we practiced our Bible verses hoping that no one else would say Jesus wept. As a few others showed up, we began when the Sunday school superintendent started us off by asking someone to open up with a song. I never had the nerve to start a song until I realized that if you openly participated, your name was written down and announced at the end of Sunday school. Everyone knew you were there because your name was called as people began to arrive at church. So I wanted to make sure that even if the people didn't hear me sing, pray, or say a Bible verse, at least they would know I participated and I was heard. Even at an early age it was possible to focus on being seen in church and not doing it for God to get the glory. I didn't realize that whatever we did while in church, we needed to make sure God got the glory and not we ourselves. Because when God gets the glory here, we will reap the benefits for being faithful to him, and pay day will come after a while.

So after the Sunday school portion was over, we awaited the beginning of the 11am service. My aunt was an elder in the church, a very powerful woman of God. She mostly sat in the pulpit during the services. So the MC announced, "The Lord is in his holy temple, let all the earth keep silent, I was glad when they said unto me, let us go into the house of the Lord. Our feet shall stand in the gates of Jerusalem" (Psalm 11:4). We were ready to begin the worship service. As the choir began to sing the opening song as they marched down the aisle, I was already trying to decide who was going to dance first and win the dancing contest for today. Whoever danced the best that day was the one that my cousins and I would mock when we got home. So it was important to me to see who would be the one to carry the trophy home for dancing during the service. Just like that, my focus for church that day was to mock someone's dance after the service, not realizing that one day I was going to understand why they were dancing. Not for a contest, but because they were dancing for a blessing that they couldn't see; a blessing that they had faith in–faith that would bring that blessing to pass. But all I saw was who was the best soloist? Who gave the best praise? Who was the best organ player? Even though I was raised in church, it took me a long time to learn the real meaning of church. Dancing and yelling wasn't the real meaning, though they play a part. Singing wasn't the real meaning of church, though it plays a part. Dressing up wasn't the real meaning of church. Being seen or recognized wasn't the real meaning. The real meaning of church is to come in and give God the glory for what he is doing and what he is going to do, giving God the praise as we waited for the blessing. It hasn't happened, but by faith it shall come to pass. Praise in advance is a praise conquering that circumstance.

After the offering plate had been passed around

twice, it was time for the dancing contest to begin. I sat back hoping the choir would sing a hot praise song. You knew the song was hitting if the piano player stopped the music and told the choir to "sing choir." After about 10 minutes of the song, the choir would stop and the show began. Usually it started in the choir and then the ushers would bring up the rear. It was a high time in the Lord, as everyone began to look at one another as the spirit filled the church, as the pastor would say. The ushers were supposed to be holding the lay members and the visitors, but they were cutting up themselves. Now I knew that we were having church because of the yelling and screaming, jumping and dancing. Not everyone was in it for the dancing contest as I was. There are many in churches that are sincere about the praise they render unto God. There are many that really fear God whole heartedly. There are some real saints who serve God seven days a week, twenty-four hours a day.

But there are some that haven't learned to be real in all they do and say for the Lord. And when you are not real with yourself, you can not be real with God. Therefore, you will live a Christian life based upon emotions. These are emotions that are high in the church while in the presence of God, but absent outside of the presence of God. These emotions are based upon the life of someone else. They can only be triggered if someone gives you a word. They are emotions that make you a needy person, always needing something to continue your Christian journey. They are emotions that cause you to depend on people instead of God. As soon as you are let down by people, your emotions won't sustain you and you will find yourself sliding back. This is all because you leaned on the emotional part of church and people and your foundation was upon them and not built upon a rock (Matthew 7:24,25). When you are depending on your emotions, dancing won't save you, shouting won't relieve you, and praying won't deliver you. This is because emotions are not stable (Joshua 1:8). God has to be first in your life in all things. Therefore, he can give you a real shout, a real praise, a real dance, a real testimony, based upon knowing God and the relationship you have with him. How is your relationship with God? Is it spiritual or emotional? Do you have a real relationship with God?

So after the choir finished, it was time for the word of God. Or shall I say time for me to go to sleep and only wake up for the benediction? I did not realize that it is the word that keeps you, saves you, delivers you and preserves you. So I slept as my spiritual food was fed to someone else who was looking for the real meaning of church and not the emotional part that I desired, not realizing that if my emotions failed me I would need something to fall back on. Without my rock, the word of God, my house was built upon sand. It was sand that would eventually dwindle away as the storms of life approached. My only anchor was my emotional feeling that I only got in the presence of people. I would find myself living off of someone else's anointing. But that was fine with me because of my ignorance. At least I learned how to shout and praise God based upon mocking my fellow Christians. So I guess my first introduction to God wasn't real beause I didn't desire to know him for myself, but because I thought it was cool to be in a praise contest each Sunday.

Allow your first introduction to God to be real and sincere. Allow God to lead and guide you (Proverbs 3:5,6). Build your foundation on the word of God. The word is a sure foundation that will not dwindle down when the storms of life are raging. When you come into God's presence being real, he will give you a praise that is not rehearsed. It will be a praise that is from your heart, and no one else can do your praise like you can. When you are real with God, emotions might leave you, but you will still stay with God. You might be happy today and sad tomorrow, but because your foundation is stable you will be able to wipe the tears and trust in God (Rev. 21:4). Come to God as you are, no strings attached, no surprises or hidden agendas. Remember he knows about you anyway. Even at your lowest point you will be able to call upon the name of the Lord, and the word shall lift and sustain you. Be real with yourself and God will be real with you.

# Chapter 2

## Learning Your Place In God:

With My Whole Heart Have I Sought Thee: O Let Me Not Wander From Thy Commandments. Thy Word Have I Hid In Mine Heart, That I Might Not Sin Against Thee (Psalm 119: 10,11).

As time passed, I grew older in the church but not in God. Many times we never reach the level that God is calling us to. We didn't allow ourselves to learn our place in God. Instead we allowed people to place us where they thought we should be. If God doesn't lift us up and put us on the level he raised us to, we will never reach our full potential. We will always depend on someone telling us where we should be. People can lift us up on a level, but the anointing comes from God. It is the real anointing that destroys the yoke (Isaiah 10:27) and that sets the captives free (Luke 4:18). It is the anointing that enables you to cast out devils and heal the sick (Matthew 10:1). It is the anointing that we will receive when we learn our place in God.

Trials and tribulations will play a major part in learning our place in God. Once we are able to go through a trial once and pass, we start to learn our place in God. It is a place based upon going through to get to the place God would have us to be, as we learn how to suffer and not take the first exit out. Every trial that we pass places us on another level in God. Every trial we pass adds a stronger anointing to our lives. Every depth of sin we walked is the same depth of holiness we must walk in. It is all right to suffer for Christ's sake (Galations 6:12).

After being in the church for a while, I decided to join the choir and see how it felt to be part of the song that caused the church to get in an uproar. I attended the choir rehearsal and was in for a surprise. Were these the same people that hosted the dance fest on Sunday mornings? The same ones that appeared to have it all right with God; the ones that appeared to have it all together in church! I asked myself how it was that they played a part in setting the tone of the church. We couldn't even agree on a soloist or the opening hymn. I began to ask myself if we were pleasing God in what we are doing. Was I ready to stand behind the pulpit and sing God's praises after arguing with other members? Sweet and bitter water can not come out of the same fountain (James 3:10,11).

So after listening to the bickering and complaining, we finally were overruled by a member that has been going to the church all of their life. You know the one! It was the one that never agrees with anyone else; the one that only uses scripture to call someone else's sins out. We finally just gave in and sang the songs this person desired. But even in our ignorance, God still blessed the service. I realized then that God loved his people so much that he would use anyone to bless them, even if they were not right with God. So after the deacon led us in prayer before we entered the church, we were ready to begin the service. The power of God moved me that day. I was officially a member of the shout fest as I gave God my praise from the choir stand. Now little children would be going home mocking me. I thought I had made it.

So I remained in the choir in spite of the confusion. Even at an early age, I realized that some things just weren't of God. So I decided to go to the elders of the church regarding my concerns. They listened and told me that "Something goes on in every church." I accepted that and it rested in my spirit. I even thought that statement was in the word quoted just like that. As time passed, I believed that more and more. I believed it so much until it was the excuse I used whenever someone would mention about leaving the ministry to go somewhere else. Therefore, I never tried to find a ministry where folks weren't bickering and talking about each other. I got used to coming in burdened from life's problems and leaving the church and leaving with church hurt. I got used to being talked about and lied about. I got used to always being misunderstood and cast down by people. Before I knew it, I was focused on pleasing people and not God. I didn't even know who I was anymore because I waited for someone to tell me who I was. I lost my identity, and when you loose your identity, it will be hard to know what God has for you to do. I didn't know my place in God. I was confused and bitter because of the way I saw saved folks acting. Since I didn't know the real power of God, I began to act just like they did. So I learned to praise God for a show. It was a show so people wouldn't know the real me; the real me that was confused and hurt. It was the real me that was sick and tired of being sick and tired. So I learned when to yell out "amen." I learned when to yell out "thank you Jesus." I learned when to shout and stomp my feet. I learned a fake praise before I was introduced to how to praise God wholeheartedly. Church had become a routine for me and not a place of deliverance and prayer. It was my emotional high for the day, and I couldn't wait to get back into the next service for my next high. I was addicted to a church high that I had to have to make it through the day.

I witnessed countless people experience the same thing I did in the church. None of us knew how to overcome it because we didn't know a way of escape. After all, there was trouble in every church. I thought the people were the same in every church. I did not realize that you can be in a place for just a season and when it is time to go it is time to go. I felt as David felt when he returned to camp and saw the enemy had come and taken his wives, money and children (1 Samuel 30:8). I felt as if the enemy had come and taken everything that mattered to me. But if it had been my enemy, I would have felt better (Psalms 55:12–14). But it was the saints that I walked into the house of God with. It was the people that were supposed to be praying for me in my time of need, the ones that held the usher positions, the deacons that prayed us into victory, the mothers that sat upon the board, and the preachers that broke the bread of life to feed me. At this point I didn't think that being saved even mattered. If I was going to be persecuted, I would be persecuted outside the church. All churches were the same according to how I had been taught. Small churches were in your business and would control you, and large churches didn't know you. Do I stay and die or leave and be on my own? I didn't know my place in God; therefore, I didn't know what to do. I didn't know who to trust, so I guess I was on my own.

I decided to pray for myself one more time before I totally gave up. Since I had only prayed like I was taught and the way I heard prayer in church, I didn't know how to begin the prayer. So I just decided to talk to God as if he was standing beside me, as if he was one of my closest friends. I began to say, "God, I am confused. I don't want to leave the church or quit being saved, but God, is it worth it? Is this how the saints are going to act in heaven? God, I can't make it on my own. I don't know enough about you to last out here in the wilderness. God, I don't even know how to give you a sincere praise that is not rehearsed. I don't know what to do, God. Help me.

At that moment something happened. I begin to cry and laid it all on the altar. I felt a wind blow on me. A new understanding came upon me. I began to understand what I had to do. I realized that I first had to get myself together and get my walk with God in line. I didn't know my place in God until I endured these trials. I realized then that I must be real with myself before I can be real with God. I must accept those things I can't change but change the things I can change. The first thing was to change myself and my relationship with God. I began to read the word and finally get some understanding so I could abide in the word of God (John 15:4). So God began to speak to me clearly after I decided to finally listen and obey. At that moment I realized that there are some things that we don't have to suffer thru. If you spend more time defending yourself to people, you are not uplifting God but yourself. Your focus is pleasing others so they can like you and put you in the in crowd on top of the church popular list. Come to yourself and remember that people don't have a hell or heaven to put you in. We are here to save others from going to hell, not to allow people to put you in or through one. If I am going to suffer, I am going to suffer because it is ordained that I go thru that trial. I don't need added trials that only benefit the people who I allow to put me through them. Remember, God will allow things to happen for you to grow in his grace and get in his will. You must be able to distinguish level trials and petty trials. Therefore, you must learn your place in God so he can tell you when you have been in that place too long. Things will happen everywhere you go, but if you never leave the dry brook, you won't know if there is another stream up the road that is flowing with blessings (1 King 17: 1–6). Don't die of spiritual malnutrition and dehydration. But live by the word in which you can drink one time and thirst no more, eat one time and hunger no more. Don't allow your fear of change to put you on a spiritual diet. Eat the word of God that will never lose its power and keep your mind focused on God.

Things do happen in all ministries, but where the spirit of the Lord is there is liberty (2 Cor. 3:17). From that day on I didn't use excuses to stay in confusion and mess in the house of God or even in my personal life. You can't stay in a mess if you expect God to bless. Learn your place in God.

# Chapter 3

## Growing Pains:

For Every One That Useth Milk Is Unskillful In The Word Of Righteousness: For He Is A Babe (Hebrews 5:13).

Now that I had experienced a few things, I thought the hard part was over. Boy was I wrong. I had just begun my journey.

As I got older my needs began to increase and grow outside what the church could fulfill. These were needs that the church wouldn't address unless you were already caught up in that particular sin. The sins of sex, uncontrollable desires, bad habits, confused sexuality, and whatever else that was good to the flesh were rarely addressed in the church.

I tried praying, fasting, working overtime to occupy my mind, and seclusion, but nothing seemed to work. I found out then that prayer will keep you but it won't satisfy you. So I tried talking about it in the church and the comments made to me were: "You just want to do your own thing," "You just want to live in the flesh," "You just don't want to be saved," "I knew you didn't want God like that anyway," and many more comments that you wouldn't expect to come from Holy Ghost filled Christians. I heard those negative things so much until I started believing those comments. So a spirit I call "what's the use" rose up in me. Why try to live holy if deep down the saints say I just want to please my flesh? After all, if the mind thinks it, you might just as well do it. So I moved on my flesh and decided to please it. Before I knew it I was partaking in sins and using scripture to back my sins up. The more I prayed the worse I got. I was at the point I didn't know what living right was anymore. I was so confused about what to do when I was caught up in a habit that the church said I wanted to be in anyway. I didn't have anyone to talk to because some saints want tell the real testimony in the church. They forget the edification of a true testimony. My problems had taken over me. I didn't realize that my problems where going to become the pieces of my blessings.

So I continued to struggle. During my struggle I continued to go to church so I could keep up appearances. I continued to sing in the choir and even give God a shout and praise. After a while my "what's the use" spirit took over again. Once sin enters in it doesn't come in alone. It brings company to ensure your demise. So I started missing church. It started with one Bible study night, then another Bible study night and a Sunday school, then a Bible study night, Sunday school morning, and now a Sunday service. Before I knew it I had missed every service that week. But I thought I was ok. Then that one week of missed services turned into two weeks, then three weeks. And in a twinkling of an eye I had missed an entire month of church. Just like that I was totally in a back sliding position and didn't realize I was sliding back so quickly.

Instead of blaming myself I begin to blame people for my spiritual destruction. I begin to say, "I don't have any money to go to church." It was excuse after excuse after excuse. Believe it or not, I started believing my excuses. Instead of getting better I got worse. My spirit got so weak I started lashing out at those who really were trying to help me. Because of hurt and disappointment from other people,

I began to think no one was on my side. I didn't realize that is where the devil wanted me to be. He wanted me to shut down and make excuses because that put me in a vulnerable position. The devil took advantage of me, and I wasn't equipped to fight him.

So I got depressed and perplexed one day. I was in the bed for days because of my depression. And those people that I pushed away were the first ones to be by my bedside. So as I laid there I began to ask God "why me" as I looked over my frail body. I had lost so much weight that you could see my ribs, and my legs were like sticks. I was in constant pain it seemed from my head to my toes. The depression was winning and I felt I was going to die. I cried out again to God, why me God, why me? It wasn't until the room cleared and I was lying in my bed and a sweet voice spoke back to me. "Why not you"? I asked the Lord, why did you allow me to get so depressed and so low? The voice spoke back and said: "I had to wait until you were in the position where you could hear me and not run away". I asked the Lord, why did you allow me to get to the point I couldn't change before I got so far from the word? The voice said: "You can't expect things to change if you keep doing them the same way". I began to cry out to God and say, "Lord, what must I do to get another chance to change"? The sweet voice said: "Come back to me." Instead of accepting the word from God, I began to play the blame game and use my famous excuses. The sweet voice spoke to me and said: "Don't be a blamer and an excuser, but be a doer, a believer, a truster, and a changer with him (God) as your guide." At that point I began to cry and surrender. I told the Lord: "Thank you for another chance." Not many days hence I began to get better. I felt myself rising up and doing the will of the Lord. By faith I saw myself up out of that bed doing the will of God. After about three weeks I was back on my feet and energized in the word of God. I began to tell God thank you for taking care of a poor sinner like me. I didn't want to ever again have to be put on my back before I listened to the spirit of the Lord.

I missed giving God a true praise. I missed being in the presence of the Lord. I missed singing so that he might get the glory. I realized that I hadn't sold out to God, but gave in to my flesh and allowed the enemy to take rule over my life. At that moment I stopped blaming the church and people and started telling myself, "You are coming out of this." So I went to church seeking God and left my problems, bad habits, and painful situations at the altar. I started seeking God and God only. Deliverance took place when my mind was made up to give Jesus my all and not just part of me. I learned the real reason to go to church all over again; to give God the glory for all the things that he has done for me. Even in the midst of my mess and mistakes, I was able to get the victory over my circumstances. I made the choice to serve God wholeheartedly. I allowed God to be the first partaker of my choices. I allowed him to order my footsteps in his word (Psalms:37:23).

So even though you go through some trials, it doesn't mean you have arrived and graduated from trial school. I had weathered a terrible storm, but there would be more waiting for me down the road. Every level you go thru is determined by how you endure your test. If you don't past the test with a 100%, you will be taking that same test again and it will be harder to past the second time around. This is an everyday journey that must be traveled carefully. There is no time to stop for a break because the enemy is waiting to take your time card so you can't clock back in. That is why you must put in overtime on this Christian journey. So when you get weak in praise, your extra praises will already be timber in heaven. Bless the Lord at all times and let his praise continually be in your mouth (Psalms 34:1). Sometimes you will leave one trial and enter into another one. As long as you endure the trials you will grow in Jesus. Grow in grace and don't stay in the same place forever in God. Your fruit will produce fruit as God purges you (St. John 15:2).

Maybe you are asking yourself how you will know when you have grown. You will know according to how you endure your trials. If you still retaliate when folks lie about you, cast you down, and dismiss you from the clique, you haven't grown. If you take the easy way out to satisfy your flesh and get out of God's will, you haven't grown. If you lose your praise because of life circumstances and tribulations, you haven't grown. If you choose to be in the clique and not please God but people, you haven't grown. If you piggy back off of someone else's anointing and pattern your walk with God behind them, you haven't grown. If you mock someone else's preaching, speaking, prophesying, singing, and never allow God to establish yours, you haven't grown. If you don't study your word and find time for God to talk to you in your secret closet for divine direction, you haven't grown. If you find yourself doing the same thing over and over again and never make a change, you haven't grown. If you are still doing just a portion of these things, you haven't grown. When you have grown, folks can come against you and you can send them a thank you card because their actions caused you to pray and you received a new anointing because of them. When you have grown, your trials and tests don't push you overboard but give you fuel to continue pushing, and you begin to sing the old song "I feel like going on." You want take the easy way out but do as the Hebrew boys did (Daniel 3rd chpt.). Even in the fire Jesus will be the man in the middle that protects and fights for you. When you have grown, your praise will be automatic. You will come in the house of prayer saying "thank you, Jesus." You'll wake up saying, "If it had not been the Lord on my side, where would I be?" (Psalms 124). You'll go on your job telling all about a man from Galilee that gave you overflowing joy when he saved your soul. You'll teach your family the importance of praying and fasting in the good times as well as the bad. You'll praise him even when you feel forsaken by death, life's problems and overwhelming situations. You have grown when your faith allows you to believe even when it seems impossible, and when you say you are more than a conquerer because you appreciated the bad so you will know how to accept and keep the good that happens to you on this journey (Romans 8:37). You have grown when you can witness and tell the goodness of Jesus to those who have prospered in their own way and don't know Jesus. You have grown when your Christian attitude exceeds your worldly attitude and you bury the old man and allow the new man to reign. When you have succeeded at these things and more, you are growing in Christ. You might not be where you want to be, but thank God you are not like you used to be. By just being real with yourself and your spiritual growth you can begin traveling the road to heaven the way God would have you do so.

# Chapter 4

## Relationships:

Jesus Saith Unto Him, I Am The Way, The Truth, And The Life: No Man Cometh Unto The Father, But By Me (St. John 14:6).

Relationships are the strongest things that can bind you to Jesus. Without a relationship with Jesus you can't reach the father (St. John 14:6). We sometimes fail to realize the importance of solid relationships. I realized that relationships with your family, your girlfriend, your co-workers, your wife, your husband, your kids, strangers, etc . . . all played a part in my relationship with Jesus. A lot of times relationships play a part in the reason why we came to Jesus in the first place. A broken heart, family hurts and pains, abandonment, and betrayal all make up relationships with someone or some thing. Before we can have a healthy relationship with Jesus we first have to know how to treat people here on earth. We have known these people, and if we can't treat them right, how can we love Jesus? If we can't get along with them down here, how will we live in the same heaven?

Family relationships play a part in many ways. Most of the time, if you have a close relationship with your immediate family, it will be somewhat easy to bond with those outside of your family. Because you know what to expect from your family, it won't surprise you when someone outside your family acts in certain ways. Because you are used to receiving love that is comforting, real, affectionate, and desiring, you won't be fooled with fake love decorated by the enemy. You will be able to keep your grip onto God. When you have that great family relationship, you have someone to fall back on when you mess up, someone to call on when you are in trouble, and someone to back you up and uphold you even when you are wrong. You know your family will be there for you. So when it comes to trusting in Jesus, you find it easier because you have experienced trust with your family. They always say a family that prays together and bonds together, they will stay together. Even in the death of family members, you can cope better because you know that you have your family to fall back on, and the one who died and left you will not be forgotten because of the family ties. You won't have any regrets because you had a chance to know them, love them, appreciate them, care for them, and live with them because of your great family relationship.

Not all families are like this. What about those that have families but are not close at all? What about those whose families are the ones that cause them to seek love and acceptance elsewhere because they didn't have it with their own family? What about those that were abused physically and mentally by their blood relationships or abused and talked about by those who should have had their backs? What about a family that desires to see them down instead of up? What about a family that gives them no support and encouragement but will be the first to bad-mouth them? What about a family where the mother wasn't a mommy? What about a family where the father wasn't a daddy? What about a family where sisters and brothers where like strangers, and aunts, uncles, and cousins were like distant relatives living miles away–a family that is only family by name and blood. These are the ones that will rely on other people not related to show them how to effectively have a relationship with God and others. They must trust someone they can't see after never being taught or never having experienced closeness of a true family. They must praise the Jesus they feel could have changed their lives but didn't. They are dying of hurt and pain but they must trust in God. They must have faith in a God that sits high when their relatives below don't even acknowledge them on their birthday. They must teach the young folks and help the teenagers and respect their elders when their own children don't respect them. They don't know where to start because they never received love, respect, appreciation, and kindness, so how can they teach what they were never taught? How can they accept what they never experienced? Their closest family relationships were with those that were of no blood relation. Their closest friend was the alcohol bottle and drug habit. Because of the desire to be loved and accepted, they respected those that were out of the household of faith. They inherited their bad habits. But at least they loved someone and thought they were loved, but could not know because they never experienced true love.

So after this you turn to the church to be that family you never had. But even there you find trouble, confusion, and pain all over again. Who can you trust? Is it worth being saved when you experience the same hurt and pain trying to live for God? How can you form a relationship with Jesus coming out of this type of experience? You've tried being real and that isn't working. What do you do?

That is when it takes Jesus to send a real saint with a real anointing that destroys every yoke (Isaiah 10:27), with the power to speak deliverance from their past and blessings to their future. These are the ones that are special to Jesus because all they have is Jesus. They are the ones Jesus can really use because they never had family to trust in, but only the family of Jesus. Their testimony alone can deliver those in similar situations and make those that have close families appreciate having a physical family to lean on. When you go without something as powerful as love, you will appreciate it when you receive it. You won't take anything for granted. When you have to go thru your trials alone without any help from people, you are empowered through your trials. You are able to encourage yourself when you get down. You are able to turn your face to the wall and say, "Jesus, come and see about me." When you have to travel life's journey alone, folks can't easily push you off your road. When they lie about you and scandalize your name, it will be like water off of a duck's back. When you experience this kind of pain and you turn it all over to Jesus, you will be like a tree planted by the rivers of water. You shall not be moved (Psalms 1:3). You will be able to appreciate your every blessing because you will realize that you could have lost your mind. You could have lost your life. You could have lost your health and strength. You realize it could have been the other way, but God had the last say. Even when you felt God had forsaken you, even when you didn't understand why you had to suffer what you suffered, when you are at your Job moment in your life, you can say, "The Lord giveth and the Lord taketh away" (Job 9:12). When you have suffered such troublesome trials and you come to Jesus, you now have a new lease on life.

Not everyone turns to Jesus. They turn to other alternatives to help them forget about their troubles. That is why it is important to be real with yourself and tell your true testimony so you can help someone else that may be going through something. You can help someone to understand that God won't put any more on you than you can bear.

Just because you don't have that relationship with your blood family doesn't mean that you can't have a relationship with Jesus. It just means that your relationship with Jesus was formed thru heartaches and pain, trials and tribulations. You realize that Jesus will take care of you. You now know that if you have Jesus you have a true family.

Relationships before marriage with your girlfriend and boyfriend play major roles if the relationship ends in marriage. A relationship should end in marriage and not begin with marriage. When we meet someone, we can not begin discussing wedding plans before we discuss having a friendship. We can't begin to try and raise someone who is already supposed to be grown. We can't force or teach someone to serve Jesus as we do. We have to begin with a friendship and allow the Holy Spirit to usher us into a deeper relationship. We as saints must teach and train even as girlfriend and boyfriend. If we want a friendship to make it to marriage, it must start with an anointed friendship. It must be a friendship based upon togetherness in the spirit and not between the sheets, a relationship not only in the church but in real life situations. If we enter into a marriage and can take care of the church affairs but not the affairs in the home, we are doing things backwards. Charity begins at home and then spreads everywhere else we go. We can't rely on the church to keep our relationships and marriages together. We must do that ourselves with the help of God. If you are taught what to say to your girlfriend or boyfriend, you won't ever be real to them because you said what you were told to say, you did what you were told to do. You didn't learn yourself through the teaching of life experiences but only what you were told. Then when the time comes and no one is there to tell you what to do, your relationship begins to diminish because you don't know what to do. If you allow people to dictate to you what you should do and say in your relationship, it isn't your relationship, it's theirs. I have heard of a village raising a child, but not of a village keeping a relationship together.

You must learn how to communicate in a relationship. Not just when you are in the spirit, but also when you are at your lowest. You are going to need someone who can catch you when you are falling in the spirit as well as in the flesh.

Many times the reason for break ups in Christian relationships is because you learned what to do in church and never
got the understanding what to do outside the church to make
your relationship work. If every time you ask your girlfriend
or boyfriend a question and they give you a church-a-fied
answer or a scripture, they could be hiding their real feelings
because they are busy telling you what you want to hear.
Ask them to be real with you. Ask them, what attracted you
to me? Why did you choose me? Do you love Jesus even if
this relationship doesn't make it? Do you love your family
and friends as well as your enemies? How do you treat others when you are upset with them? What do you want in life
and what can you offer that will improve my life? How high
is your tolerance level when you are broke and angry? What
do you think about change? Can you adapt even when things
are not going the way you planned? How do you treat a little
sister or brother who is not your blood? How do you treat
those that you say you love? How do you treat the ones you
dislike? Do you believe in setting goals and working towards
them? How do you handle life pressures? Do you believe in
paying your bills before the due date? What do you do when
you don't have the money to pay the bill? Do you feel life
or people owe you something? How do you respond to your
sickness or sickness with other people? How do you handle
pain, strife and being lied about? When you are knocked
down by circumstances, how do you get back up? Can you
tell me your real testimony without leaving out parts? Can
you pray for me when I don't feel the need to pray? Do you
really trust in Jesus even when trouble is brewing on every
life side? Can you catch me if I fall and not complain about
my weight? How do you feel a family should be, and what
do you do to make it the way Jesus ordained it to be? When
these questions and more have been asked, you take their
answers to Jesus before you accept them and wait on an

answer from above. When Jesus tells you what to do and you listen, others opinions won't matter because you heard from on high. Make sure you can answer these questions before you ask your girlfriend or boyfriend, because it starts with you being real with yourself before you can be real to anyone else. If you both give similar answers from God above, you are on your way to a successful relationship that will end in marriage. Start a relationship right by "just being real."

You can't only be Christian in the church house; you must also have a real mentality on the job. Even on the job you have relationships with your fellow co-workers. Normally you spend more time on your job with co-workers than you will with your family. They get to see you more hours of the day than the ones you are staying with at home. Co-workers will see the side of you outside of the saints. They get to hear how you talk, see how you walk, and know how you handle different situations under all kinds of pressure. Some co-workers even begin to feel like family because you will find yourself confiding in them about your most personal thoughts. How we act on the job will determine if we can draw souls from our employment because they get to see the real you. Do we invite them to our church? Can you serve the same Jesus in church as on the job? Your co-workers can be your biggest critics or they can be your biggest supporters. Yet you have to treat them as Christ would whether they are your friends or your enemies.

Co-workers can be some of the most influential people in your life whether it is a good or bad influence. They can encourage you to press through trials or encourage you to take the easy way out. By spending so much time with them on the job, it is easy to pick up their habits, their way of talking, even their way of thinking. You have to be able to determine what advice to accept and what advice to shun. You have to be able to know when to laugh, when to joke, when to be serious, and when to stand on God's word. If you are going to be respected by them, you have to make sure you go about this the Godly way. The best way to do that is start off being real and true to God and yourself, and then you can act accordingly around your co-workers.

It is very easy to get pulled into a clique on the job and not even know how you got there. Before you know it you are labeled along with the rest of your co-workers when it might not be your real personality. Always remember you start out the way you want to end up. If you want to earn respect, you must stand for something or you will settle for anything. Treat your co-workers the way you want to be treated. Be careful how you entertain them or allow them to entertain you. Don't allow the good that you do to be tainted by someone speaking evil against it. If your co-worker can't stand the ground you walk on, you continue to pray for them according to Psalms 37. Believe me, they will need you one day, to ask you for a favor or even to pray for them. Allow the life you live to speak for you.

When you portray this persona from the beginning, if you are promoted over them they will respect you even more. If they decide to buck against you, you continue to stand on the word, and God will fight your battles and make your enemy be at peace with you. But it is not as easy as it sounds to do so. You can easily find yourself doing what you do just to be liked by everyone, being pulled in every direction, trying to make everyone happy and pleased with you. Before you know it you won't know who you are because you are being too many different people to please everybody. You realize then that everyone is not going to like you. You are not going to be able to please everybody. Everyone is not going to agree with you and support you. They will even try and dig a ditch for you and hope you fall in. As the saying goes, "They better dig two because the trap they set will be for them instead of you." You will lose friends and associates along the way, but you will gain respect from them because you stood on the word. When you stand on the word of God on your job, you will be respected as a man or woman of God. You will find yourself being more than just a co-worker. You will be a friend, a counselor, a mediator, a teacher, a role model, and most of all, saved by standing on the word, all because you were real with your co-workers from the beginning of your relationship with them.

After learning how to form good relationships with those that I knew, I had to learn how to also have a relationship with strangers. Now this I learned the hard way. I remember traveling on the road one day and I passed by a couple who were fussing and fighting. There was no one on the block that day except for them and me. As I approached the couple, the argument went to the extreme. I wanted to say something, but I remembered being told to mind my business and stay out of domestic disputes that don't concern me. So as I passed the couple, I heard a loud slap, and then another, and another. I wanted to turn back but I just kept walking. I then heard the lady begin to scream, "Help me, help me, please sir, help me." I was scared to death, but I turned around. The man yelled out, "Mind your business, mind your business." So I turned around and began to walk away and I heard three more slaps. The lady yelled at the top of her lungs for help. I looked around, and it seemed as if no one was on the street or that block but me. I began to pray, Lord, what must I do? The Lord spoke back to me and said; "Feed my sheep" (John 21:16). I began to tell God, "I don't think I have the food she is looking for." The Lord spoke back and said, "Feed my sheep." At that moment I reached for my cell phone and called 911 as I approached the couple. The man looked up and told me once again to mind my business. I responded back, "This sheep is my business." He pushed the lady down on the ground and headed towards me. Before he could get to me, a police car finally came around the corner and the lady got up and ran towards the car. The man looked at me and took off running. The cops ran him down and finally caught him after a long foot chase. I walked over to the lady, as her face was bruised and bloody, to make sure she was alright. She looked up at me with her swollen eyes and responded, "Thanks for saving me." I haven't been acknowledged as a person in years until today, and by a stranger." I turned and wiped the tears from my eyes and headed back towards my car. I felt good that I helped someone outside the church house, outside of my peers, my co-workers, and outside of my family. I didn't know whether I was going to see her or him again. One day I went to a revival on a Tuesday night about three months later. As I stood there worshipping God, I felt a tap on my right shoulder. I turned around to see who it was. I didn't quite recognize her because I had only seen her beaten up, battered and bruised. She asked me, "Do you remember me?" I replied, "I don't think so." She said, "I am the stranger whose life you saved that day on the street." As I burst into tears, I gave her a hug and asked her how she had been. She replied, "Fine, I was saved right after that terrible ordeal." She stated, "I have been praying to God to allow me to see the stranger that saved my life and led me to God." She stated that as she was being beaten by the man that stated he loved her, she was praying for God to save and deliver her from this abusive relationship. And God did just that. She said she had been serving God every since and thanking him for a second chance. We both hugged each other and got back into the service. After the service was over, she told me thank you again, and I told her to continue holding on to God's unchanging hand. She replied, "Who wouldn't serve a God as good as ours?" As we went our separate ways, I realized I still didn't get her name. I ran out to the parking lot and she was nowhere to be found. I didn't tell her to repeat the sinner's prayer. I didn't read the Bible to her. I didn't invite her to church or a Bible study. I just acknowledged a stranger in need. I fed a lost sheep that was being devoured by a wolf. I never saw her again, but I knew I had made a friend by helping a stranger. I learned to not focus on making friends, but being a friend.

We must be careful how we walk by strangers. We never know if we are entertaining an angel or not. How many times do we stand beside someone in a check-out line and never speak or even acknowledge that someone is standing beside us? How many times have we sat beside someone at a function or even in church and not asked their name? How quickly do we judge someone by what they are wearing, how they talk, the color of their skin, their economic background, where they live, or even what we have heard about them? We never give them a chance to become anything more than a stranger. We forget that the harvest is plentiful but the laborers are few (Matthew 9:37).

Yes, there are precautions to take before you approach people due to the condition of the world. We must continue to trust in God and be led by his holy spirit. The spirit will tell us what to do, what to say, and how far to go. We must reach outside of ourselves to reach those who want to change but don't know how. We must persuade men and women to come to Christ as Paul did in Romans chapter 8. No one wants to have blood on their hands because they didn't reach out to others as Christ reached out to us. Trust in the Lord and lean not to our own understanding, and acknowledge God in all of our ways according to Proverbs the third chapter.

So the next time you see someone's car broken down on the side of the road as you head to your place of worship; the next time you are standing beside someone in the check out line; the next time you are sitting next to a stranger in church, doctors office, function, concert, etc . . . just look at them and acknowledge them. You will be surprised at how one word or acknowledgement can help a person. Remember, we all are strangers to someone, but now we are heirs of the throne of Christ (Galatians 3:29). Spread the wealth; there is plenty to go around for everyone.

To have a effective relationship with Christ, it is important to have a good relationship with your spouse. Many times we find it easy to minister at the church and to others and neglect ministering in your own home. It is very easy to get out of the will of God, especially when you are nice and helpful at church but helpless when you are at home. You are now out of God's will. Charity starts at home and then spreads abroad and covers a multitude of sins (1 Peter 4:8). That is why Jesus said love your wife as Christ loves the church (Ephesians 5:25). Before you know it, you will be able to give advice and counseling outside the house and forsake your family at home, able to help other families but forsake your own wife and kids. You will begin to compliment other people's spouses and haven't even complimented your own. You will speak kind words to other peoples spouses when you haven't said a kind word to your own in days and sometimes weeks. Yet we will dedicate ourselves to the church when we really need to go back and do our first work over (Revelation 2:5). We can't put our focus on others, and our family relationship diminishes.

We will begin to rebuke the enemy in the church and the enemy will move into our home. We will find ourselves blinded to the fact, and we will become two different people traveling down two different roads. One spouse will be in the church and the other at home, all because they don't want to go to the same place of worship with someone who isn't real at home. They are helpful to other peoples spouses and children and neglectful to their own at home. They carry a powerful anointing in the church, but they lack that same anointing at home when they are praying for their spouse and children at home. For these very reasons the divorce rate is so high right in the church and among those that are confessing Christ. If you want to experience a powerful move of God using you in the church and elsewhere, let your work begin at home.

Minister to your spouse at home and don't wait until you are in the presence of others to flatter your spouse so they can go back and want the same thing from their spouse. Tell them how good they look before you get to service, so when others compliment them, they can say, "Thank you, my spouse said the same thing." Let them know this every day so when you do compliment someone else, your spouse won't be rolling his or her eyes at you. Teach your kids at home as if you were teaching Sunday school in the church. When a bond is formed in the home, that same power can flow in the church. Where two and three are gathered in Jesus name, Jesus will be in their midst (Matthew 18:20).

There will be times when tests and trials will come. The enemy will try and come in and destroy your household. But no man can enter into a strong man's house and spoil his goods, except he will first bind the strong man; and then he will spoil his house(Mark 3:27). When spouses are on one accord, they can see trouble coming before it arises. They see trouble concerning their kids, loved ones, family members, problems, etc. Their discerning spirit will be turned on at all times, ready to rebuke and call those things that are not as they should be. This is all because your relationship with your spouse and kids is on a solid foundation built upon the word of God that started at home and then spread abroad.

In the church it is good to have good relationships. The Bible teaches us to know those that labor among us (1 Thessalonians 5:12). Love one another in the church. Get rid of your judgmental spirit according to St. Matthew the 7th chapter. Do not assume that a person doesn't know God like you do just because he or she doesn't praise God as you do. Do not assume they are backsliding just because you don't see them in a church service. Do not assume something is spiritually wrong just because their smile is not as wide as yours. We do suffer through things outside of the church. It is not always the devil doing something to us. Don't give the enemy all that credit. Allow your discerning spirit, the one from God, to lead and guide you and tell you what to say to people in your church. The greatest hurt a person can go through is a church hurt. One of the main reasons people lose interest in going to church is because of poor relationship with the members of the church.

When a person get saved they expect the church members to accept them as they are and to teach them as they travel on their Christian journey. Many times this is not the case. We must shape and mold people to be like Christ, and not our personal version and opinion of Christ. Because of hurt feelings and church meetings about childish stuff, they are pushed out of the church. We don't realize that a church hurt can scar one for life. That is not the will of God. God designed the church to be a house of prayer where the sick can be healed, delivered and set free from the chains of bondage. It is designed to be a place where we meet for fellowship and give our God the honor and the glory for the things he has done.

Be obedient to leadership in the church, especially if the leadership is following Christ according to the word of God. Support your fellow members and the building of the church and ministry. Support your pastor's visions, for the people perish without a vision. Don't allow the enemy to tear down the fellowship in the church. Don't allow the enemy to destroy your relationship with your fellow members. Don't allow denominations to detour you from serving God just because you believe differently. Remember, we are serving and praising the same God.

The enemy has crept into the church, causing the members to be scared to fellowship because they are afraid of being hurt. Past pains caused by churches and so-called saints can cause people to stay out of church and not believe that people can change. They feel that if they are going to be mistreated in church, why go? You will begin to feel those outside the church treat you better than the saints in the church. We wonder why we can't persuade people to come to Christ and go to church. It is all because the enemy has divided the people and relationships are not built upon the word of God. They are built upon secret agendas, personal gains, status quo, cliques, and economic backgrounds. The enemy will allow them to think they are right and they will use the word to justify why they do what they do. THE DEVIL IS A LIAR!!! When real saints realize they can't grow in that type of ministry they leave, only to be ridiculed and cast down for leaving before they lost their faith completely. They are again told that something goes on in every church. If you go to a large ministry, you are told the pastor won't know your name. If you go to a small ministry, you are told it will always be confusion because everyone knows everybody. If you belong to a large ministry, you are told you go there because you are trying to hide your sins. You attend a small ministry because that is where your family goes. The reality is that God is everywhere. He is in the small ministries and he is in the large ministries. When you have a relationship with God built upon the word, the spirit will lead and guide you and you will plant your feet in the church where you can grow spiritually. Be real in the church and with your fellow church members. Being real will help form healthy relationships in the church and every part of your life.

# Chapter 5

## Accepting The Call Of God:

But Now Thus Saith The Lord That Created Thee, O Jacob, And He That Formed Thee, O Israel, Fear Not: For I Have Redeemed Thee, I Have Called Thee By Thy Name; Thou Art Mine (Isaiah 43:1).

I remember belonging to a ministry that was growing and striving in the will of God. People were joining after feeling the power of God moving in the church. People were joining after witnessing the power of God perform miracles before their eyes. I was the choir director, an Elder, Sunday school teacher, and even on the praise team. God was using me in every way. I was respected and used in the ministry. So I couldn't say that I wasn't being used or that I was being looked over. Yet something was missing in my spiritual life. It was a void that I couldn't explain, but I was thirsting for something and it wasn't being quenched. So I continued in the ministry and waited upon the Lord to order my footsteps. I continued to preach and prophesize, and many people were blessed through the ministry that God had placed me in. But after the service, after the moving of the holy spirit, I still felt that void. I tried to discuss my problem with different church members and friends. They would give me their opinions so much that I allowed their opinions to become fact in my spiritual walk. Many times when we don't want to face the truth and get in God's will, we will agree with others before hearing from God.

So I continued in the ministry, and soon things began to happen. Small things began to happen in the ministry, and the enemy would blow them out of proportion to the point of having meetings to resolve them. My singing and preaching began to change. I wasn't focusing on pleasing the people and spiritual leaders of the church. I was tuned into God and God only. Therefore, the members began to misunderstand me, not because I didn't make the word plain, but because they weren't used to me preaching and teaching on that level. That is when I realized that I had gotten comfortable in the place I was and I didn't want to move from that place. It is easy to get complacent because you are in your comfort zone and you don't want to move out of it. You are not ready for change so you just stay there. Little did I know that when you are called by God, you have to stay in God's will. You are going to have to move when he says move. You are going to have to speak when God says speak. But I still didn't want to move.

As I continued in the ministry, things began to get worse. Before I knew it, I spent all my time trying to prove to others why I did this, and why I said that, why I didn't agree with this, why I didn't go to that, why I felt it should have been done this way, and on and on and on. I was spending more time defending myself instead of doing God's will. Even my family didn't understand what was going on with me. Even I didn't understand; I couldn't explain it. The majority of the time, if you don't understand what God is doing, then you know you are in God's will. If we understood everything that was going on in our life, we wouldn't fast and pray. We wouldn't seek God for answers because we would already know and wouldn't need the Lord to speak to us. But that still wasn't enough for me, so I stayed in the ministry.

About a month down the road I couldn't even concentrate while in church. Things continued to get out of hand. Remember, when you are not in God's will, you are opening the door to hell and telling the enemy to come in and wreak havoc. The trouble left the church and got into my house. And if your house isn't in line, you can't get the church in line. It all starts at home and then spreads abroad. Trouble was all around me on every side. I cried out with a loud voice and surrendered my all unto God. I told the Lord, I can't take anymore, but Lord, you know all things. I told the Lord to lead and guide me and I would follow his voice. The trouble was just too much for me to bear. I couldn't even talk to my wife because we weren't on the same accord. It got to the point that her opinion didn't matter to me. I would listen to the opinion of the church members instead of her. I had put her on the backburner in my life. I was totally turning away from her and running to the church when the answer was in my house. Anytime your house is not in order and you are happier in church then at home you have problems, especially when God has surely joined you and your spouse together and the Lord has told you to stay there and support and listen to your spouse. I knew when I began to neglect my family that the enemy was spoiling my house.

So I cried out again to the Lord for direction. The Lord replied to me, "Hearken to the voice of your wife." It was then that I realized something. Don't let anyone talk bad to you about your spouse, and don't you talk bad to anyone about your spouse, because your tongue has the power to speak life or death. We must be careful what we say and what we receive from others (James 1: 19,26, 27). My wife told me that "You have done all that the Lord has instructed you to do in this ministry and it is time for you to go." So I listened to my wife and I knew it was the Lord using her to set us both free.

So I went back to church and told the pastor and

leaders what the Lord was leading me to do. Boy was that a mistake. I thought everyone was going to be supportive and encouraging. I went from being respected to being ridiculed. My church family decimated quickly and in a hurry. It is amazing where your friends and family run to when you really need them. The encouraging phone calls stopped. My wife began to get discouraged. I was amazed at the responses I got from church going, God fearing people; all because I wanted to be in the will of the Lord. It was then that I realized that if the Lord tells you to do something, don't try to explain to everyone why you did it because they just might talk you out of getting in God's will. Go to your pastor, ask for guidance, and allow the Lord to lead you and then "JUST DO IT" under the leadership of the Holy Spirit.

I went through a hurting period for about two months. I was at the point that I just wanted to go back to please people so I could have friends again, so I could have church stardom again, so I could have church recognition again, but I didn't. I would rather be in God's will than please people that have no hell or heaven to put me in. The Lord revealed to me that he puts certain people in our lives for a reason, to help us stay in his will. When it is time to move on he will put more people in our lives to help us get there in a timely fashion. So I accepted my calling to another level and went about my Father's business.

When I got in God's will, things began to happen that made me think I had missed my calling. I felt I was just throwing money out the window. Trials and financial problems came from everywhere. But the Lord kept saying to me, "It is going to work out, just trust in me." So I held on to that saying, and even today I live by that saying. Things always get worse before they get better. The darkest hour of night is just before the break of dawn. So I kept on praying and believing that things would change, even to the point that I said if things don't change, I will still believe and trust in God (Daniel 3: 16, 17, 18). Well, things didn't get better right away. As timed passed by, I fell in the worst financial difficulty I had ever been in. I had to downsize the vehicle I was driving, from a brand new car to a car almost ten years old. My wife and I had to sell our nice, large home because we just couldn't keep up with the Joneses anymore. I couldn't understand why I was going through what I was going through, but I knew I had to stay in God's will. I couldn't see down the road, but I still kept the faith and I knew I was in God's will.

So we moved in a smaller home in a different neighborhood. I wasn't excited about the move because it wasn't as glamorous as what I was used to. But I held on to my faith and I knew things were going to work out somehow. After we got settled in our new home and in our older cars, things began to come together. God had to strip us of the comfort zone. Then he had to put us in a lower economic level so we could appreciate our blessings when he blesses us back a hundredfold of what we lost. He had to put us in a position so we could bless others financially without us giving away our bill money. Once we were settled and our finances were loosed by God, we were able to give to others and plant seeds in different ministries—all because we got in the will of God. You are not truly blessed until you can bless someone else. I finally understood it because I went thru it first. Experience is the best teacher. I was finally on the right path and in God's will. If you are saved and a tither, a giver, there is no way you will stay in the same position and same financial status if you are in God's will. You must learn to properly budget and spend the money you are making before God will give you a whole lot of money. You have got to be a good steward over what you have now before God can give you more. Because if you can't tithe with what you are paying out, you are living above your means.

I lost friends, family members, and church support, but I found my way back to God's will. It is worth losing those things as long as you are in God's will. When your family and loved ones forsake you, the Lord will take you up. He will send you sincere friends. He will send you to a church where you can grow and lean on him to make it. He will send you to a church where you are respected even if you are not on the praise team, singing in the choir, or preaching in the pulpit. You don't have to be in the spotlight to be a star with God. God will restore the years the cankerworms and caterpillars ate away (Joel 2: 25). This is all because you are in God's will and you trust God to order your footsteps. Be obedient to the spirit and move when the Lord tells you to. When you are in God's will, everything that you do will have a positive impact on something or somebody; in your home, your church, your job, in the streets, the grocery store, or wherever you are. You will learn to give God praise in the bad and in the good and you won't complain during the trial. Your testimony will edify everyone that hears it. You will be able to save people on the brink of suicide, people who desire to throw in life's towel, when they hear your testimony. By telling your testimony, you will be able to reach people who don't know God for the pardon of their sins. You will be able to lead them to repentance. Your testimony will help people who knew God, but lost their faith because of pain and suffering. When you get in God's will, you will be able to help many people—all because you surrendered your will for God's will. When you are real with yourself, you can love what you do for the Lord and do it well as you are led by the Lord. You have accepted the call of God.

# Chapter 6

## Following First, Then Leading:

And He Left The Oxen, And Ran After Elijah, And Said, Let Me, I Pray Thee, Kiss My Father And My Mother, And Then I Will Follow Thee (1 Kings 19: 20).

Now that I had begun to travel the right road, I knew it was time to find my Elijah to lead me where I needed to be. I knew that I needed a covering over me that my ministry might be blessed. I needed someone anointed to pray for me, someone to see trouble before I did and give me a fair warning so I could rebuke the enemy. So I began to seek out a ministry that was truly ordained by God. I prayed to God to order my footsteps in his word and direct my path (Psalms 37: 23). I knew that my leader had to be strong in the Lord. I knew that my leader had to be able to cast out devils, lay hands on the sick and the sick be healed. My leader had to be a person that stands on the word of God and nothing else; a leader that had suffered and gone thru some trials and came out victorious. I needed a leader that has prospered even as their soul had prospered (3 John 1:2). So that is what I was seeking in a leader, a leader that was following Jesus and carrying out his work. I knew that before I could lead anyone, I had to be a good follower.

So I prayed and asked God to help me understand how to be a follower first. The first step was to find a leader that was going after the things of God. Many times we find ourselves following someone that isn't going after anything or is pursuing the wrong things. Those types of leaders will play off of your emotions by making you feel good for the moment. They never help you get healed of your transgressions, but instead they put a bandage over the wound. The highpoint of their church service is seeing you jump up and down and dance along with the music. There is nothing wrong with praising God. But why not praise God because you have the victory and not because the music moves you? When you are following someone that is after the things of God, they will help you chase the enemy out of your life. Anytime you are going after something, you have to leave something behind. A real leader will help and teach you to lay aside every weight that doth so easily beset you (Hebrews 12:1). A true leader will be able to encourage and teach you to not only lay aside the weight, but to destroy it so you will never pick it up again. A true leader will not sugar coat the word to pacify your feelings to keep you as a member. A true leader is more concerned about your soul. A true leader don't desire to have your blood on his or her hands because he or she didn't lead you the right way. A true leader will help you to decide on what you need to go after, and when you reach your destination you will know how to stay there and still be in the will of God. True leadership will teach you so that you can pray for yourself, lay hands on yourself, rebuke the enemy yourself, and cancel the assignment of the enemy, all because you have learned how to follow true leadership. A true leader will teach you how to get up and try again if you fall along the way. Repent if you have to, as long as you don't take your eyes off the prize (Philippians 3:14). Be a good follower and go after the things of God.

When you are pursuing the things of God, you have got to be a good listener. You must be able to accept direction. Before you can do that, you must be able to listen. When people don't want to listen, you find them never grasping onto the things of God. They have decided to have their own agenda and not listen to the man or woman of God set aside to guide them. When we don't listen and accept direction, we find ourselves in a dangerous position. We begin to think that we are right and everyone else is wrong, all because we wouldn't listen. That is why we have churches on every corner; they decided to do their own thing because they wouldn't listen to their leader. And we wonder why their church doesn't grow. It will not grow because the leaf left the tree before it was completed, and now the leaf is withering because it doesn't have a source of life to tap into. Instead of apologizing and getting it right, we continue to go down the wrong road and even attempt to lead others down the same road. Just because we don't listen to a good leader, we have to go to great limits to keep the people that are following us. We know that we reap what we sow, so we have to make sure that our followers never see the real us. So then you begin to water down the word to fit your situation. You use the word to beat down instead of building up your followers, and you put them in a weak state of mind to control them (2Chronicles 33:6). This is all because you wouldn't listen and didn't have enough humbleness to just say, "I am sorry." Even the best leader must be able to say, "I am sorry." And don't sugar coat it by saying, "IF I offended you, please forgive me." There is no IF; just apologize so you can get back on the right road and pursue the things of God. Listening is very important to being a good follower.

Now that we are learning how to pursue the things of God, we must go to the next level of being a good follower. We have to learn to support the men and women of God that we are following. We support them not by just paying our tithes and giving offerings. We support them by helping them to rebuke the enemy. Don't let anyone talk bad about or condemn your leader. Give no place to the devil. When we go along with the leader, we will have the leader's back in all aspects. We won't mind bringing them a glass of water or carrying the leader brief case or even being a doorkeeper for the leader.(Psalms 84:10). We will call and pray for the leader without calling and asking for prayer for ourself. We will allow the the leader to pass down his or her mantle to us that we might continue to carry and convey the word of God. Even greater things will we be able to do just because we learned to follow first and be a good servant to the man or woman of God. Support the leader when they go out to preach across the land. Go when you can, and when you can't, send up a prayer of support. When you support your leader God will rain his blessings down on you. Anytime you bless others, God will give you double for your trouble. Support them by following them in good times and in bad times. Stand by the leader when the going gets rough and it seems the enemy is winning. Support and go along with him or her when it seems you are going by yourself. Anything that is ordained by God will stand and the Lord will lift up a standard against the enemy (Isaiah 59:19). When you support a good and true leader, you will receive a double portion of his or her anointing even as Elisha did from Elijah (2 Kings 2:9), all because you supported the man or woman of God. Your greatest support will come from living the life you confess to him or her. Be real with the man or woman of God and he or she will be real with you.

After being submissive to the man or woman of God, you will be elevated to a higher level with a stronger anointing—all because you learned to follow first. You won't have to mock them because when you are a good follower, God will give you your own unique anointing. Your leader will be glad to say that you are a chip off the old block and that you turned out all right. Your results will be gigantic. You will be blessed and receive the gifts of God. You will be able to teach as you were taught, lead as you were led, and more, but with the anointing God gave you for being a good follower. You will be able to draw souls and lead them to Christ because you took the time to learn, listen, and follow; therefore, your ministry will be blessed. Your results will be your leader giving you his or her blessing and allowing you to carry the word just as he or she did without jealousy, envy, or strife.

Last but not least, when you are a good follower, God will complete you. This simply means you are ready to be a leader. You are now whole, finished, and equipped to lead. When you are a good follower, you can do the things of God and not worry about failing because you are complete. You did things the way the Lord instructed you to do them. Doubt will not cause you to be double minded (James 1:8). You are complete and ready to go out and proclaim the gospel as you were taught, and with a new found anointing. You are a leader that learned how to follow first. You are a leader that learned to submit first. You are a leader that learned to listen first. You are a leader that learned to support others before you ask for support for yourself. You are a leader that learned to go after the things of God by following a good leader. You are a leader that learned to put God first and do as you were taught and not do what you thought. Now that you have learned to follow first, you can teach others to do the same. You wont have to worry about support from people because you will get the support. If you don't, you will continue standing and preaching the word of God. You won't have to worry about being a pastor and controlling the members because you are scared they are going to rebel against you. But you are complete, all because you learned to follow first before you led anyone.

Now that you have learned to follow it is time to

lead. A good leader has to be able to direct the people in the way that God is leading he or she. Therefore, a leader must have a vision so he or she will know what direction to take (Proverbs 29:18). You can not lead anyone if you don't know where you are going. You may not understand how it is going to work out or when it shall be done, but you will know the direction to lead. Direction is important. A good leader must know how to read life's map. A good leader will ask for direction if he or she find themselves lost. He or She won't go miles and miles the wrong way. He or She will go to God and wait on an answer before they continue going down the wrong road. A good leader will have the ability to appoint people in the position they should be in to help he or she lead others. They will surround themselves with people that share the same vision. And if the people don't see the vision that the leader is seeing, they will still support him or her because they know their leader was a good follower therefore they trust the leader's direction. A good leader will know who is for him or her and who isn't. Paul was being followed by the damsel that was possessed by a spirit. When Paul got tired of the spirit, not the damsel, he cast it out. You need good people around you to help you carry out God's plan for you and the people following you (Acts 16:16, 17). Direction is needed, and by being a good follower, God will grant you the ability to go in the right direction and to point others in the right direction.

When you are a good leader, you will possess the power to persuade people to come to Christ (II Corinthians 5:11). You will not allow the enemy to talk against the word of God to you. You will have the ability to show people the way into the arms of God. You will have the ability to lead them to repentance and on the road to salvation. You have to be planted and steadfast to be able to persuade men and women to come to Christ. You have to know that you know, that you know, that you know, that you are a child of the king. You have to know this so that you can tell others the benefits of being saved and living holy. You have to be a doctor that is confident in his or her ability to prescribe medicine to heal the body. If a doctor is not confident in his or her work or practice he or she will prescribe the wrong medicine and could cause someone to lose his or her life or get worse than he or she is. A doctor does not want a malpractice lawsuit. Therefore, doctors have to know that they know what they are doing before going in the medical field, just as a good leader must know how to lead and persuade men and women to come to Christ. If they don't know how, that blood of that innocent soul will be on their hand, and that is the worst malpractice lawsuit ever, so good leaders must know how to persuade and lead people to the throne of grace.

A good leader must be ahead of his or her followers. He or she must be one step ahead of them to be able to tell them what lies in the path. A good leader must be able to use his or her spiritual eyes to look into the future and rebuke the past of the enemy so the people will be safe. He or she must be strong even when he or she feels weak because he or she has someone looking up to him or her expectantly. A good leader must not allow things to affect him or her and knock him or her down. If a follower sees that the leader can't withstand trials, tests, and tribulations, he or she will be reluctant to follow. A good leader must be able to hide the tears until he or she go in their secret closet to talk to the Lord above. The followers must see a strong leader at all times. One mistake could be devastating to those that are following you. Allow your testimony to edify others after you have come out and been delivered. A good leader must be able to withstand the storm, the winds, the lightening that life brings, so that even when the leader reaches the breaking point he or she will be able to hold it together. You might bend, but you won't break. Then you can warn the people what is ahead to prepare them for the test. And by a good leader having the ability to look ahead, you can tell your followers the victorious outcome. This will allow them to trust in you even more because they witnessed you standing on the word of God in the good times and the bad times, the happy times and the sad times, just like children that have no worries at all, because they don't see their parents struggling to put meals on the table and clothes on their backs. All they remember is having three meals a day and clean clothes to wear. And if they saw their parents struggling, the parents didn't complain but they thanked God for it being as well as it is. This is how a good leader must be in order to lead the people and teach them how to suffer. For the song writer said, "If I suffer for Christ I will gain eternal life." (When I see Jesus, Amen.)

A good leader prepares the road for others to follow even after he or she are gone. When you are a good leader you won't have to tell the world how and who you are. Your life will speak for you. A good leader's life will prepare the road for his or her children and family. A good leader will be remembered years after he or she is gone. The legacy of a good leader will live on and continue to positively affect people as he or she travels life's road. When a good leader prepares the road, the road might not have a lot of travelers, but those that travel the road will be real to themselves and real with God. When a good leader prepares a road, he or she will not put any rest stops on the road. We don't have time to stop and take breaks and allow the enemy to catch us unguarded. We will always keep on the whole armor of God at all times (Ephesians 6:11) so that we will be able to withstand the wiles of the devil. Therefore we don't have time to stop and take breaks. A good leader that prepares the way will put grab bars on the road. So if you should happen to fall along the way, you can reach up and grab onto the grab bar and pull yourself up. The grab bars are the word of God. We won't need first aid kits because the word will heal you even while you are running the race (Isaiah Chapter. 53). For God will wipe all tears from your eyes and take away the pain (Revelation 21:4). When you are a good leader you will die in peace because you know you have prepared the road that will save many lost souls.

So be real and true to yourself. Then you can be a good follower. And when you are a good follower you are destined to be a good leader. So follow first and then lead.

# Chapter 7

## Your Choices, Your Mistakes:

And If It Seem Evil Unto You To Serve The Lord, Choose You This Day Whom Ye Will Serve; Whether The Gods Which Your Fathers Served That Were On The Other Side Of The Flood, Or The Gods Of The Amorites, In Whose Land Ye Dwell: But As For Me And My House We Will Serve The Lord (Joshua 24:15).

With all of God's awesome power, he still gives us the power to choose. He gives the ability adversely to decide what our destiny will be by simply making a choice, the ability to decide how our past will not affect our future, and the ability to cancel our future by a choice we made. He gives the power to determine how far our ministry will go all depending on the choice we make, and the power to decide whether we are going to obey God's word by making a choice. Choice is a gift that even God doesn't have to give you. This power is in our hand to use as we choose–the power of choice. Because of the power of choice, we are in the situation we are in now. Whether it was a good choice or a bad choice, we still made the decision to choose what we chose. Regardless of the outcome or what comes after we made the choice, we still made that choice. Now we have to live with our choice. Choose–the thing that we have the power to do. Choice, the power that even God allows us to use at our will.

What are your choices? What are choices that you

have made that you regret? What choices have you made that you are proud of? What choices have you made that have allowed you to prosper and grow? What choices have you made that have caused your growth to be stunted? What are the choices you have made that have allowed you to never reach the potential you could have? Can you come out of a bad choice and land back on your feet? Can you simply change a bad choice? Can you be trusted to make a choice and not blame anyone else for the choice you made? Do you know the difference from a good choice and a bad choice? Do you make your choices or does someone else make them for you? Are you capable of making a choice? Do you make choices without thinking about them or the outcome after you make them? Do you make choices regardless of who your choice might affect? Do you own up to your choice when something bad happens from the choice you made? Choices, choices, choices. There are many questions; there are many answers, all because of the choice we made. Make sure you make the right ones.

How do you make a right choice? How do you make a wrong choice? The first step in making a choice is counting up the cost before the choice is made to determine if you are willing to pay the price. Find out if it is worth making that choice. Research your choice to see if the choice is going to be beneficial or regretful to you. Find out why you even have to make a choice. Most of all, can you live with the choice you have made? Be real with yourself so that after you have made the choice, you can only blame yourself for the outcome. Your choice can lead to good, bad, happy, or sad results. Which result do you want?

When we choose a mate, what made us choose that person? Were we led by the holy spirit to make that choice? Or did we make the choice because that is what we wanted? Did we think it over and count up the cost before we made the choice? Or did we make the choice because of the way we were feeling at the time? Our mind was made up and nothing and nobody was going to change our mind, not even God. Now that you have made your choice, what comes next? When we choose a mate, we are saying this person will be equally responsible for how our future will be. We are saying this person will be equally tied to our destiny and our accomplishments. We are agreeing that this person will be strong where we are weak. We are saying this person will have our back when no one else does. We are saying that this person will help us grow into a positive future with you and your children. We are saying this person will help you balance your check book and increase your bank account. Will our choice in mates be all that we were expecting them to be, or will we be disappointed in our choice? Either way we have already made the choice. Now you have to deal with it. Since God wasn't in the choice, you are out there on a limb by yourself. Now you must suffer the consequences whether good or bad. Don't overlook the signs and still make a choice that you will regret. What is done in the dark has a way of coming to the light. If your mate is already acting the fool, there is a possibility that they will get worse. If your choice is caught up in a bad habit and there are no signs they are going to drop the habit, think about it. Don't make the choice in hope they will change afterwards. Wait and see if your choice is going to get there self together. If your choice is already forgetting that he or she isn't in this thing by them self you need to rethink your choice. If your choice already has existing choices, you need to rethink your choice. If your choice is below your expectations, why do you think he or she will ever reach your expectations? If your choice was someone else's choice before you, why do you think that your choice is ever going to make you his or her only choice? If your choice hasn't accomplished anything in life before, are you sure he or she will accomplish anything after you choose them? If your choice don't respect his or her parents, do you think your choice will respect your parents or even you? If your choice can't get along with his or her family, do you think they will get along with yours? If your choice curses the woman or man out in the drive thru, will he or she curse you out? If your choice disrespects the check out lady, will your choice disrespect you in public? If your choice don't take care of his or her children, do you think he or she will take care of your children? If your choice never saw a good father and mother, will he or she know how to be a good father or mother? If your choice has never experienced true love, will he or she know when they are truly being loved by you? If your choice doesn't know how to show appreciation now, will he or she show it later? If your choice is boring and without excitement now, will he or she be boring and without excitement later? Be real with yourself so you can make the right choice, because after the choice is made and it turns out to be bad, we now must choose to stay with the choice or get out. Now we have a problem. How do we get out of the choice we made? How long do we stay before we choose to make another choice? Well, even that is your choice. Once again you must count up the cost. If you choose to stay, will you be able to stay sane? If you stay with your choice, whose life will be affected? If you stay, can you continue to accept what your choice is doing? If you stay, can you affectively continue doing the will of God? If you choose to stay, can you afford to? If you stay, will you ever reach and accomplish your goals? If you choose to stay, you can't blame the devil or anyone else but yourself for the choice you made. If you choose to stay will you have to work harder or hardly work? If you choose to stay, can you say after all is said and done, it was worth it? If you choose to stay, will you regret it after looking back over your life and your choice? Either way you still are the one that has to make the choice and live with it.

Do we make choices to make us happy or for our well being? Even a child has a choice when it comes to which parent they want to live with during a divorce or separation. He or she has the power to choose for happiness or for their well being. What is good to us isn't necessarily good for us. What makes us happy now may not keep us happy later. Do our choices make us happy for the moment and sad the rest of the time? Do we choose the job or occupation because it makes us happy or because of our well being? Will this job be beneficial to our future and those in our future? Will this job be better for your well being and ruin your happiness? Is it worth choosing a job that brings the money home even though you can't enjoy the home or the money? Is it worth choosing a job that when you leave you have to take medications to be able to return? Count up the cost and see if your choice in jobs will pay off.

When you choose a house, a car or any material thing, have you counted up the cost? Will you choose a house that is more than you need because you can? Do you choose a house because someone else has a similar house? Do you choose a house to have a high appearance for people? Do you choose a car that will benefit your family and finances? Do you choose a car because you need a car that reflects the house you stay in? Do you choose a car because you want to out shine the family down the street? Do you choose to spend before you make the money, or do you choose to spend because of want or need? Do you choose to spend because you can, do you choose to spend instead of saving? Do you choose to spend and not save for a rainy day or an unexpected expenditure? Do you choose to spend now and worry about it another time? Whatever our choice is, it is still the choice we chose to make. Whenever you have to make a decision about your spending or finances in general, make sure you have counted up the cost. Make sure you have looked at all avenues and outcomes. Don't spend for now and forget about later because your future will have financial decisions as well as your past and present. Make the right choice.

When you are making a choice, consider your selection of choices–in other words what you have to choose from. Don't just limit yourself because you chose from what you knew about instead of researching and broadening your selection. If you choose from what you have always chosen from, you will always get what you have always chosen, and you will have the same outcome because of the choices you are making. You can't expect things to change if you keep doing them the same way. If your choices have put you in a rut, start choosing something different. Don't settle for less when there are so many choices to choose from. Make a list of things that you desire to happen to help you before you make the choice. Make a list of expectations first and then choose according to your list. Don't make a choice because you were told to. Don't make a choice because that is what your parents did. Don't make a choice because you want to make someone else happy and forget about yourself. Remember, you will have to live with the choice you have made. This goes for a mate, job, house, family, etc. Select from a good selection. Select from a selection that you have researched and not one that has been researched for you. You must make the decision and determine when, where, and how you want your selection to be. You have the right and power to make your choice. You play the greatest part of all in your decisions. You must make the choice, so be sure you make the right selection. It's your choice.

Many times our choices will result in mistakes. Once we realize that we have made a mistake, we must live with it. We have to accept the fact that we made the mistake and no one else made it but us. It is not what you do when you make the mistake; it is what you do after you made the mistake. Will this mistake stop you from making correct decisions and choices in the future? Will you allow this mistake to kill your desire to get up and try again? Will you allow this mistake to stop you? Will you allow this mistake to stop you from living a prosperous life? Will you allow this mistake to kill your accomplishments and destroy your goals? Will you lie down in defeat because of a mistake or get up, dust yourself off and keep on trucking down life's road? You must tell yourself, "I messed up, but I won't give up." You may have made a wrong decision that caused mistakes, but take away the mis from mistake and TAKE another chance. We all will make mistakes but some of us will not allow that mistake to determine our destiny. If you have made a mistake by choice or failure, you are human, but you are not defeated. Just learn from your mistakes so you won't make the same one over and over.

Sometimes you make mistakes because you don't understand or because you perceive something wrong (Proverbs 4:7). You must understand how you made the mistake so you will not make it again. If you choose to do something that has a negative affect on you after you do it, you won't stop doing it until you understand that doing this will cause problems for you. If a policeman stops you three days in a row for not wearing your seatbelt and gives you a ticket each time, even though you don't like to wear your seatbelt, you will because you now understand why you are being stopped. So you wear the seatbelt.

Understanding why you made the mistake will not always stop you from making the same mistake. A lot of us do things that we know are morally wrong and can cause harm to others as well as ourselves, but we continue to do them over and over again. Why? Because it feels good. We can have the right perception, but the desire of feeling good overrides what we perceive. Therefore, we end up making more mistakes. Just because it makes us smile, laugh, feel sexy, feel desirable, and wanted doesn't mean it is good for us. We understand why we shouldn't do or say it, but we can't stop ourselves because of the way the mistake makes us feel. Whenever something makes us feel good in the way we desire, we forget about what is morally right. We forget about trying to avoid making the same mistake. All that is irrelevant to us. We just want to feel good. Whenever a mistake can take us to a place that we want to go even though we can only stay a little while, you have got to deal with a big mistake. The longer we continue to make that mistake, the greater the mistake becomes. The mistake has now become a part of our life. The mistake has become a necessity to us. We must make this mistake or we feel as if we are going to die. Our perception is, I must do this thing or I can't go on. Now you must pray that the mistake is corrected before it is too late.

The only way to stop making this "feel good" mistake is to understand why you must stop. If you make a mistake and don't learn anything from it, you will probably make that mistake again. But when you understand why you must stop, you can begin to change the outcome of the mistake. If your mistake gives you a temporary high or good feeling for just a moment, that isn't worth the high. Why settle for something temporary when you can achieve and pursue something definite? If your mistake causes you to loose control to someone else or something that causes regret after the fact, you need to drop that mistake. If your mistake causes others danger as well as yourself, you need to drop that mistake. If your mistake changes you into a person that you weren't before you make the mistake, you need to drop that mistake.

If your mistake makes your body feel good for a moment but can harm your body later, you need to rethink making that same mistake. If your mistake causes you more harm than good and more disappointment, more sadness and pain, more regret and attitude, then you need to revisit the choice you made. If your mistake feels good to make now but can haunt you years down the road, you need to count up the cost to continue making this mistake. It is good to feel good, but it is even better to feel good when you didn't make a mistake to get that feeling.

Learn from your mistakes. Allow your mistakes to teach you. Take control of your mistakes; don't allow your mistakes to take control of you. Understand why you made the mistake. Don't allow your mistake to remove your understanding. Grow from your mistakes. Don't allow your mistakes to stop you from growing. Teach others not to make the same mistakes you made. Don't allow your mistakes to stop you from warning someone else heading down the same road. Be proud to admit you made a mistake so you can begin to correct it. Don't allow your mistake to stop you from admitting you are making a mistake. Be real with yourself so that when you make a choice or a mistake, you and only you will have the power to correct the choice and correct the mistake. Your choices, your mistakes will determine how your life will turn out.

# Chapter 8

## My Feet Are Planted, No Turning Back:

And He Shall Be Like A Tree Planted By The Rivers Of Water, That Bringeth Forth His Fruit In His Season; His Leaf Also Shall Not Wither; And Whatsoever He Doeth Shall Prosper (Psalms 1:3).

I am reminded of the story of Shadrack, Meshach, and Abed-nego (Daniel 3chpt.), how in spite of a threat to be thrown in a fiery furnace, they stood and trusted in God. Their feet were planted and they weren't going to turn back even if it cost them their lives. Even though they saw the fire before them, they stood still because they knew that God was God alone. When the enemy tossed them in the furnace, Jesus met them there in the midst of the fire. Are we planted in Jesus as these boys were? Will we turn back when the fire is in front of us? Will we turn back when we get in the fire?

When you are planted, you can't move on your own. You must depend on what you are planted in to provide you with everything you need. Therefore, you have to trust what you are planted in. When you are planted you are put in the ground to grow. You are not put in the ground to lay prostate and stay in the same position without change. If you don't grow, you need to check and see what you are planted in. Is it fertile ground? How often are you fed? If you don't get the right food you will soon wither and die. Therefore, we must be careful and make sure we are really planted and receiving the right nutrition to survive and grow.

When you are planted, you will not be able to uproot at will. You will not be able to leave the ground and survive even if you try to put yourself back in the same place you uprooted from. Once you uproot, you have lost many needed nutrients to survive. Therefore, your possibility of death has increased because you disconnected from your source (St. John 15 Chpt.). We as Christians can't be in and out of the word and expect to survive this Christian race. We will not be able to draw anyone else if we are not stable ourselves. We can't be planted today and unplanted tomorrow. We can't be nice today and mean tomorrow. We must be the same each day, and we will if we are planted in the right ground. Even if the wind blows, the lightening flashes, and the fire rages, we will be able to hold our ground because we are planted. We might bend, but we won't break. I am reminded of a very cold winter. An ice storm had come and the trees were loaded down with ice. Some trees were so loaded that the weight of the ice caused them to tumble over and break in two. The ice was so heavy that when the tree fell over, the roots came completely out of the ground. The tree was planted, but not deep enough to sustain a storm. As I continued to travel the road, I saw a tree that was leaning completely over, almost level to the ground. The tree was bent over as if it was going to break at any time. But when I looked at the roots of the tree, the roots were deep into the ground and had a firm foundation. The tree was able to stay planted because of the deepness of the roots. When the ice melted away, the tree stood up taller than ever because it was deeply rooted. Many of us must be like this tree. You will go through things in life. You will have to endure terrible trials. You will have to suffer through some things. You will have to deal with sickness. You will have to deal with being talked about, pushed aside, picked out to be picked on, and left alone, but like the tree that was bent over almost level to the ground, you can stand as long as you are planted in God. Life will weigh you down to the point that you can't stand any longer. You can't face the world because of the weight of your problems and because of the pain that you are going through. After a while you don't even understand what is going on and why you have to go through it. You begin to ask, why should you have to endure this trial and not someone else? You will begin to feel you are doing all you can to live holy and yet you are being dealt these trials and tribulations. It just isn't fair is what you will begin to say. You will begin to ask, "What is wrong with me?" Why must I go thru this? If God cared, why did he put me through this? But if you hold out, all things work together for the good of them that love the Lord (Romans 8: 28). After a while the sun will shine. The ice and weight of your trial will begin to melt away, and after the ice and weight have dissolved, you will stand taller than ever before. You will have a testimony to share with the world. You can tell the world, I was bent almost level to the ground, but I didn't break and my feet are firmly planted in the Lord.

As I continued down that road, I saw trees that were bent over, but because their roots were wrapped around another tree they were able to stand. By grabbing on to another tree that was better rooted, they were now living off of one support system. If the tree that is planted firmly, don't soon cut off the tree that isn't; both trees could soon fall. The next storm or wind could easily blow them both over. Even though one of them is rooted, the roots are not designed to hold them both up. Have you ever seen yourself in this position, trying to stay planted and having to hold up someone else that is pulling you down? How long do you hold them up? That will depend on if they want to be planted in the same ground you are. If they desire to be planted as you are for the good, you must try and hold them up until help comes. Your source will see that you need more nutrients and supply you what you need. This will make you able to keep someone from falling that desires to stand but just doesn't know how. You will help hold them up, and soon help will arrive. After the ice had melted away, I saw men out in the woods straightening up a tree that had almost uprooted but was leaning on another tree. The men took the tree, sat it up, and replanted it's roots back in the ground. Not only did the men save the tree that had fallen, but they also restored the tree that was holding the fallen tree up. The tree that had fallen had another chance to plant itself deeper in the source to prevent this from happening again. One tree saved another tree until the fallen tree got help. We as Christians can learn from these trees. Don't be quick to allow someone to fall by giving up on them. If you are rooted, you will be able to help someone that isn't or someone that isn't rooted deep enough. Hold your sister or brother up. You might bend, but you won't break.

I remember meeting a lady one day that was testifying to another lady about how she would never turn her back on God. As she was telling the lady her testimony, everyone around her was crying and listening as if they were being delivered as the lady told her testimony. The testimony was so powerful because she didn't hold back. She was real with her testimony and because she was real, people could relate and desired to hear more. After listening to the lady's testimony, I realized that many people would have given up if they had to endure those types of trials. Why would we trust a God that allowed us to endure such things as this lady had to endure? But this lady said that even at an early age her feet were firmly planted and there was no turning back. This is how her testimony went:

She began by saying that even as a child she began to endure life's pain. She stated that she remembered having a dream of a man carrying her across a beautiful field of flowers as she rested upon his shoulders. She later found out that man in the dream was her father. This was the only memory she had of her father because that was the last time she saw him in life. He died and she never got a chance to experience life with him. She never got to know how it felt to grow up with a positive male figure in her life. She never experienced a father telling her that she was beautiful and teaching her what men to watch out for. There was no father teaching her how a real man should treat her and what she didn't have to accept, teaching her what sayings to look for coming from a conniving man. She had to figure it out on her own.

Life didn't get any easier after that. As she grew up, she didn't remember a happy childhood. She remembered being picked on by other kids to the point she spent more time crying than smiling. She remembered being beaten up by the neighborhood kids, thrown through windows, glass doors, and off four foot porches. Even after that, she would stand in the mirror and tell herself that she was beautiful as she wiped the blood from her body. One day as the neighborhood kids were getting ready to beat her up again, she decided to fight back. She jumped on the leader of the group and fought her heart out. Once the fight was over, all the kids just ran away. She had proved to them that she would not accept abuse and get used to it. At that point she realized that fighting might not be the answer, but she didn't have to take the abuse. She said that if you make up your mind to change something that is hindering your life, you can do it even if it takes getting beaten up. She never was taunted by those neighborhood kids again because they now respected her, all because she took a stand.

She begin to tell us how she was over at a cousin's house one day. Her cousin was older than she was but she still visited her cousin. Her cousin happened to have friends over that day. They were drinking and having a good time. She was only 12 years old. She went to one of the bedrooms to lie down. As she was lying there, a friend of the family came in the room. He closed the door and proceeded to the bed. She stated that she tried to get out of the room, but it was as if the room became a small closet with no exit. As the friend of the family took away something she would never be able to regain, she felt as if she was worth nothing. The next day she ran to her mom to tell her what had happened. Her mom told her that it didn't happen and she had to forget it right then. Her mom never took her to the hospital to have her checked out. A year passed, and one day she woke up with pains in her stomach. She ran to her mom and her mom took her to the hospital. Turns out she had an STD and because it had not been treated, it left her unable to have her own kids. Instead of her mom comforting her, her mom never said a word. She didn't get the love and support from her mom and was left to her own devices.

One day as she was getting out of school and returning home, she walked thru the door and couldn't find her mom. She waited for her mom to return, but her mom never did. She went over to her kin folk's house and asked if they had seen her mom. They reported they hadn't seen her. She asked if she could stay with them until her mom returned. Sad to say, they refused and didn't allow her to stay. So she left at the age of 13 in tears and without a mom, a dad, no guidance, and she was left to her own devices. Since she couldn't pay the rent, she found herself staying in abandoned apartments and sleeping over at friends' houses until their parents found out. She had to go back and climb through windows of abandoned buildings to have a place to lay her head. If she wanted to have a nice night of rest with heat and running water, she had to give her body to men that only wanted her for one thing. So she found herself on the wrong road living a promiscuous life; that was when she was introduced to drugs and alcohol. She found refuge in them because they helped her escape her reality. Since she didn't have any guidance, she found herself on this road for 4 years. One day she woke up and didn't recognize the person she was lying next to or remember how she got there. She arose and left with her dignity still intact. She decided that she was better than that and began to make a change. An old neighborhood lady took her in until she could get on her feet. She found a job paying minimum wage and managed to save enough money to get her own place at the age of 17. She stated it felt good to be able to come home to a warm place and not have to do anything she didn't want to. She had overcome again and managed to plant her feet once again. She decided she wasn't going to turn back and would never go through that part of her life again.

As she continued her testimony, she began to tell them that one day on the way to work she met this older man. They hit it off from the start. She decided she wanted to spend the rest of her life with him. The relationship was going great. For the first time she was happy and felt that she was getting ready to live some good days. Good days were something that she hadn't really experienced. She felt she finally could get the family she never had. One day as she returned home from work, she noticed that the T.V. and radio were missing. She waited for her man to return home. When he walked in she questioned him about the missing items. He told her he pawned them to support his drug addiction. She was devastated again. But because she wanted to be happy and make it work, she stayed in the relationship in hopes things would change. Well, she stayed for 5 years and things got worse. Once again she found herself saying she deserved better than that. She planted her feet once again, left that situation and never returned. Once again she conquered a trial and there was no turning back for her.

She found another place to live and began her life over again. She received word that her grandmother and uncle had passed in the same week, so her family decided to have a double funeral. She realized this was her mother's brother and her mother's mother. She hadn't seen her mother in years, since the morning she left to go to school years ago. Even in her pain because of the loss of her grandmother and uncle, she still hoped to see her mother show up to the double funeral. Well, she didn't show, so once again a hope of rekindling her relationship with her mother was gone. But she squared her feet and continued standing.

She decided to attend a cook-out given by the lady that took her in. At this cook out she met a young man that was staring at her the entire time. They were introduced, but she never saw him again until about three months later. They began to date and after a short engagement they were married. Then, even though she wasn't supposed to be able to have kids, God blessed her and her husband with twins. She had finally received the family she desired. It was a long time coming, but she finally got what she wanted and never had.

She began to end her testimony as everyone stood around in tears. She told them that even through the storms of life and all she had been through, she still had joy. After all she had been through, she hoped for the best. She told them to plant their feet in a firm foundation and whatever life may bring, don't allow it to turn you back. After her testimony was over, women and men began to cry and fall down upon the altar. They began to admit things that had happened to them in their pasts, and God brought deliverance in the house. People began to repent and change their lives all because of this lady's testimony. All because her feet were firmly planted. Even though the enemy uprooted her during her life, she always found her roots and source again. Now her roots are deeper than ever and there is no turning back for her.

We must all learn from this testimony. In order to stand in the midst of storms, we must be firmly planted in the right ground based upon the word of God. The ground will supply you the nutrients you need to fight off the enemy and withstand the storms of life. Once we are planted to this magnitude, no matter what comes our way, we will not turn back, but we will look to the hills from whence cometh our help (Psalms 121:1). Your feet will be planted and there will be no turning back. Be real. Tell your real testimony. The testimony will help others that are afraid to admit they have done things they are not proud of. Most of the time people want to change, but they just need some guidance on how to do it. If you are rooted and planted in God, you should be able to help someone else. If people know that you have been through something and you are still standing, that will encourage them to stand and not turn back. Tell your real testimony whether it is about childhood hurts, marriage, divorce, drugs, alcohol, loneliness, rejection, peer pressure, church hurts, decision making, poverty, wealth, abuse, neglect, secrets, lies, etc. If you confess, God is faithful to forgive (James 5:16, 1 John 1:9). Plant your feet in the word of God. Be like a tree planted by the rivers. Don't be moved. Once you are planted there will be no turning back.

# Chapter 9

## Your Faith, Your Fears:

Now Faith Is The Substance Of Things Hoped For, The Evidence Of Things Not Seen (Hebrews 11:1).

For God Hath Not Given Us The Spirit Of Fear; But Of Power, And Of Love, And Of A Sound Mind (2 Timothy 1:7).

Faith is a word that has unlimited powers if used in the right way. Faith means to believe in something so dearly that regardless of the circumstances, you still continue to believe that it will come to pass. The Bible tells us to have faith the size of a mustard seed and you can move mountains (St. Matthew 17:20). By just believing in something, you can change the outcome whether you are saved or a sinner. The power of faith can cause you to hold on to dreams that haven't come to pass, but you continue to believe in spite of the situation. You must have faith to the point that if it doesn't come to pass, you still have faith in God just as the Hebrew boys did in Daniel the third chapter. If God didn't bring deliverance to them, they still believed that he had the power to do so. Because of their faith, God didn't deliver them out of the fire but while they were in the fire. Their faith caused them to believe even to the point that they were near death. So the Hebrew boys were safe either way, all because they had faith in God. Do we possess this kind of faith as the Hebrew boys did? Do we stand on God's word in spite of our circumstances? Do we allow our fear to take over our faith and cause us to speak doubt?

Faith and fear are one and the same. Having faith will cause you to believe in something, and negativity won't override your faith. Fear will cause you to look at what you are missing out on while you are believing and waiting. Fear will cause you to always expect the worst and only speak negative things. When fear takes over, you will only be able to see what your eyes see. You will never be able to see beyond your problems, your situations, or your circumstances. You will never be able to hope for anything because your lack of faith will not allow you to. Life has a way of causing you to have faith or fear. Which will you choose?

Is it easy to have faith or fear? You must make a choice and decide which one you want. Abraham decided to have faith in God and not fear losing his son (Genesis 22 Chapter). Even though Abraham loved his son, he loved God more. So he decided to lay aside his fear of losing his son and trusted God. Abraham knew that the Lord would provide. Because of his faith, he built the altar to sacrifice his son Isaac. As Abraham was lowering his knife to kill his son, the voice of God stopped him and directed him to another offering instead of his son. So in spite of Abraham's fear, his faith overrode the fear, and God provided as Abraham believed that he would.

But there will be times that even having faith will not change your situation, and fear will have nothing to do with it. I am reminded of a great man of God. A man that had great faith in all situations in spite of what the problem might be or look like. He was traveling and preaching God's word from city to city. The sick would call on him to come and pray for them. He would believe what the word said and God would show up every time. This man of God would pray for the cancer patients and the Lord would move the cancer and leave the doctors wondering what happened. He would pray for those that were vexed with HIV. The patient would go back to the doctor, the virus would no longer be in their blood stream, and the doctors would be amazed at the progress the patient made in a small amount of time. This man of God could speak a word over the telephone to someone and that person's situation improved almost instantly. The Lord used him to prophesize to many people, and it would come to pass just as he would say. The Lord had granted him the power to cast out devils, and he had a powerful spirit to discern good and evil. He was known as a man of faith and many depended on him to pray for them that they might be delivered. Then after all this man of God had seen and witnessed to prove that God was God, fear somehow came in. One day he was at work and got a call that his father had a stroke and a heart attack and was rushed to the hospital. The young man didn't get upset because he knew that God was going to heal his father and make things all right. When he arrived, the doctor pulled him outside and told him his father's discases were going to win and his father was going to die. The doctor even told him that he and his siblings were probably going to suffer the same things their father did. The man of God told the doctor that the "DEVIL WAS A LIAR" and his father was going to live and not die. The man of God continued to speak the word of God as he fasted and prayed. He anointed his father and prayed for him endlessly. He just knew that God was going to deliver his father from this sickness. During the sickness, his father had given his life to Jesus and began to believe that God was able to deliver him. The man of God just knew that God was going to move because he had faith and so did his father. One day the man of God went to work, and around 12pm he received a phone call telling him to get to the hospital because his father had gotten worse over night. He still had faith that things were going to be OK. The man of God arrived at the hospital and was told to go to a waiting room. He noticed that a lot of family members were there also. After being there for about 30 minutes, a doctor came in the room. The doctor kneeled down on his knees and said that his father had had another heart attack and didn't make it. Like a brick slamming down on his head, he covered his face as he ran through the hospital in tears. This powerful man of God couldn't understand why God didn't heal his father. He couldn't understand why after praying for so many others who were delivered, why didn't God answer that one prayer for him? He was devastated and began to ask himself, why did this happen? Did he lose faith and fear took over and he didn't realize it? The man of God began to ask himself, did he lose his faith? Where did he lose his faith? When did fear come in and choke his faith to death? At that moment, fear came into his life and faith slowly moved out. Because of his father's death, he began to doubt the powers of God. When he was called upon to pray for others, he just said a rehearsed prayer to please the people he was praying for. He began to make excuses for why God didn't bring deliverance to people instead of standing on God's word. He had lost his faith. All because he was afraid that he would tell someone what God would do and feared that it wouldn't come to pass. So he began to play it safe. His faith was gone. Fear had taken over.

The man of God continued on this path for about two years until one day his son fell sick. He had to make a choice. Would he allow the death of his father to cause him to never have faith again? Would he say a rehearsed prayer for his son and not believe that God would really deliver? Would his fear cause him to have all his hope in man and not in God? When he arrived at the hospital, he looked upon his son, who was lying there hurting and crying. At that moment, he became furious at the devil and his works. He began to rebuke the enemy out of himself before he could rebuke it out of his son. He spoke to fear and cursed it, and called upon the power of God that had been promised to him by the Lord. Once he had regained his faith, he began to speak healing words over his son. When he spoke the words, he spoke them with power and authority and decreed the healing of God over his son. Within an hour his son was healed, and he was released from the hospital the next day.

It took an experience with his father's death for him to regain his faith and conquer fear. To this day, he is standing on God's word with faith, even if God doesn't do what he asked. He still believes that God can do all things, and he is passing that same word on to others.

Maybe you had a situation such as the man of God. Or maybe you had another situation that caused fear to choke the life out of your faith. You only believe in what you saw and not those things hoped for. Regain your divine faith by believing that all things work together for the good of those that love the Lord and are called for his purpose (Romans 8:28). You may not see it, but just believe that terrible thing that happened to you is going to work out for your good. Even though the man of God lost his father, the death caused him to change his diet, to exercise, and to continue to rebuke that generational curse from passing down any longer. You may not see a change, but allow faith to be your eyes. The things you are hoping for will be your focus and goal. You will be able to set your face like a flint and not be moved, and you will stand on your faith as your faith stand on your fear (Isaiah 50:7).

Don't allow your fear to cause you to lose your faith and miss out on a blessing. Many times we desire things, pray for things, seek things, but we are afraid to step out to get those things. We will say we have faith, but fear will cause us not to reach out and grasp onto what God has for us. It is just like telling God you want to change something in your life but continuing to do the same thing day after day. You never made a step to do something different, therefore your situation stayed the same. You have the faith, but fear won't allow you to use your faith. So you talk about something that you will never make a step to accomplish because fear has paralyzed you. For this reason, a lot of people stay at the same job, in the same state, in the same church, in the same relationships, go to the same places, and more–all because their faith has been choked by fear. Your mind is telling you to have faith and step out, but your heart over-rules your mind because of the fear of change. So you just stay there. If Elijah would have stayed at the brook after the water had dried up, he would have died of thirst (1 Kings 17:7). He obeyed God, and when it was time to move he did. Many of us have stayed too long and the brook has dried up. But because of fear, we stay there and inhale the dust of a past blessing. We allow our fear to kill our faith, and we miss out on a blessing. Many people have done this with jobs, relationships, businesses, churches, situations, etc.

The only way we can avoid sitting at the dry brook is to go where there has been rain. Do research before you make decisions on anything. Weigh the pros and the cons. Pray and fast about an answer and move when God says go. Don't just sit around and wait for God to drop the blessing in your lap. God will do what we can't do after we have done all we can do for ourselves. Make a step to achieve that which God has for us through walking by faith and not by sight (Habakkuk 2:4). You must know when the brook is dried up so you can move on to your next destination where there is plenty to eat and drink. God will send the right people in your path to give you what you need to reach your destination if you walk in faith.

I am reminded of a swimmer telling his testimony. He stated that he and his friend used to love to swim. They were only five feet tall but they would swim in any water, regardless of the depth. They both were good swimmers and dreamed of swimming in the Olympics one day. They would even teach others to swim and encourage them to make swimming a part of their life. They would swim during the summer, spring, fall, and winter. It didn't matter what the temperature was. They would swim because they loved it. Well, one day the friends were swimming at the beach on a hot summer day. They had gone as far out as 50 feet from the shore. All of a sudden one of the friends was overtaken by a wave and began to sink to the bottom of the ocean. Even though he was a good swimmer, he could not overpower the waves. He began to panic. When fear took over, he suddenly forgot all that he had learned about swimming and was slowly drowning. The other friend saw him but didn't believe he was in trouble because his friend was a better swimmer than he was. But when he saw his friend go down and not come back up, he rushed to his aid. He went under water and grabbed his friend and swam back to the shore. The life guard met them and assisted bringing his friend to shore. They performed mouth to mouth resuscitation and revived his friend. When his friend came to, he was scared out of his mind. His friend declared that day that he would never swim again, and advised his friend to give up swimming along with him. Because of fear, both friends gave up swimming; one, because of a near death experience, and the other because fear was planted in him. They both lost their faith in swimming and decided to give up the sport forever. Now the friend that nearly drowned was glad to give up the sport, but the friend that saved him had doubts about giving up something he loved and desired to have a future in. So he decided to tell his friend that he was going to start swimming again. When he told his friend, his friend was furious and declared that if he swam, he was never going to speak to him again. His friend told him that just because it happened to him didn't mean it was going to happen to him also. His friend then told him that since he taught him how to swim and was the better swimmer, it would happen to him. But the friend didn't allow his friend's fear to overtake his faith of swimming. So he walked out of his friend's room in disappointment because his friend wouldn't support him. But his faith overrode his fear and the fear of his friend, and he began to swim again. One day as he was swimming in college, an Olympic scout had heard about him and decided to come to the college to check him out. By the friend conquering his fear and not allowing his friend's fear to overtake him, he continued to practice so he could achieve his goal one day. The scout loved him and saw Olympic gold potential. The scout approached him and offered him a chance to try out for the Olympics. He accepted the challenge and couldn't wait to tell his friend. Once he told his friend about his chance of a lifetime, the fearful friend began to rejoice with him. Through rejoicing for his friend, his own faith began to come back. So they both left and went swimming in the same water that almost took his life. Once he conquered his fear of swimming, they both tried out for the Olympics. The scout was impressed with the both of them and they both made the Olympic swim team. Fear slowed down the progress of one friend, but the other friend conquered his fear by having faith. Because one conquered his fear, his faith took them both into their blessing and a lifelong dream came to pass.

There are going to be times when problems, trials, tribulations, and circumstances cause you to lose faith and allow fear to take over. There will be times when those closest to you will plant fear in you and cause you to lose faith. But by having a firm foundation in God, your faith will not disappear for long. What God has for you is for you if you believe and have faith, even if you have to go about it by yourself. Once the enemy realizes that you have immovable faith, he can't plague you with fear. Your faith will stand and fight your fear, and it will give you the faith to go back and help those that have helped you but have lost their faith. Because they had one day planted a seed of faith, when their fear overtook them, God allowed them to reap what they had sown. One friend's faith helped to conquer another friends fear. With faith all things are possible. Allow your faith to stand with others in your home, job, church, marriage, circumstances and trials. When you get weak and begin to loose faith, God will sustain you so that you can sustain them.

We can overcome many things by just believing that God can change things for our good. Even if it doesn't come to pass, you still will believe that God had the power to make it so. Continue to be real with yourself. You will not always believe and have faith in all situations. You will not always inherit fear if something doesn't work out for you. It is your choice to make, to have faith or to have fear. Choose faith over fear. You have the power to conquer fear in all your life endeavors (Read Hebrews 11 Chapter). Choose this day to have faith to conquer all your fears.

# Chapter 10

## I've Learned To Just Be Real:

And The King Said Unto Him, How Many Times Shall I Adjure Thee That Thou Tell Me Nothing But That Which Is True In The Name Of The Lord? (1 Kings 22:16).

Once we have reached the level of being true and real with ourselves, the real Christian journey begins. Now that we have laid aside every weight that has slowed us, we are able to pursue the things of God wholeheartedly (Hebrews 12:1). When we are able to be real with ourselves, we can pattern ourselves even more after Jesus. Our lives will become fact and not fiction. A fiction lived life can appear to be true and even told that all may believe. A fiction lived life that is not based upon truth can be lived so long that even the storyteller will begin to believe the stories. People are easily more entertained by fiction than by the truth. Once your life has flowed over into fiction, you will find yourself no longer being real but living life in a fairy tale, not only spiritual but naturally also. You will not be able to determine what steps you should take in your life because you were never real enough with yourself. Therefore, every step you take has to be told to you by someone else. You were unable to be led by God because you didn't know how to be real with him.

The first step to come out of a fiction lived life is to admit your faults so that God can help you be delivered. If you are perplexed by a habit, don't hide the habit when you are around certain people. Before you know it, you will be living a lie because you hid your habit from them, and now you think it is ok. You will find yourself being someone else when in the company of certain people. You will be leading a double life, all because you didn't want them to know the real you. Remember, people don't have a hell or heaven to send you too. Only you can determine where you spend eternity. Don't duck and dodge, hiding a habit. What is done in the darkness will eventually come to the light, and you will be exposed (Luke 12:3). If you are real with God he will come in and bring deliverance. But you first must be real enough to admit your habit. Then you must want to stop the habit. Be real, either hot or cold (Revelation 3:15). Don't bind yourself by not being real with yourself and real with God. Don't live a fictional life.

When you are real with yourself, you will be immovable. Nothing or nobody will be able to move you out of your place in God. You will be able to stand adversity on every hand. Because you are real with yourself, you will know what you are capable of doing. Nobody will be able to speak anything negative over your life and cause you to lose ground, all because you know who you are. You are real. When you are real, you will know how to talk to people and what to allow people to say to you. You won't have to wait for people to approve of you because you will know who you are. Confusion will not cloud your mind when it comes to making decisions about your life. You will be able to think clearly and make the right decisions. You will be able to stand on a firm foundation not only with God but with decisions, your job, your family, etc. You will be steadfast and able to stand in all that life may bring. You won't change your mind easily after talking with people. You won't start something today and stop tomorrow. You will fulfill your destiny because your faith will not allow you to waver. You will be consistent with yourself and with God.

Life circumstances will determine if you are going to be real. When you are first introduced to God, at that moment you must decide if you are going to be faithful to his word and faithful to yourself. At that moment you must decide if you are going to be like other people or establish your own personal relationship with God. Will you base your religious beliefs on what you are told, or will you study to show yourself approved (2 Timothy 2:15)? Will your walk with God be real or rehearsed? Will your praise be more entertainment than sincere? Will you praise God because you can or you must? Will you praise him even in the midst of a trial? If you are not real, you will inherit a praise instead of God birthing one in you. You will be able to look around during service and see that you are praising God like everyone else with the same dance and the same shout. When you are not real with yourself, you will not be able to give God true worship. You will look around and find yourself sounding like everyone else when you begin to speak in unknown tongues. Your prayer language will be inherited and not birthed from God. We all are unique. There is no one else like us. Therefore, you are an original. When you are real, you will be able to grow into the person that God has ordained you to be–a unique, original, all because you are real with yourself first and then God.

When you are real, you will be able to stand in the place God has called you. You will be able to stand in that place even when hell has broken loose on every side. Because you are determined to stand for God, you will not be moved. You will know where God has called you, and you will fulfill your destiny because you know your place. You will be able to endure the growing pains of life, all because you are real.

God is calling us to a higher place in him. We are living in the last days. The Bible is being fulfilled every day, and it is evident that the end is near. We don't have time to play around with our salvation. Life is getting shorter and shorter each day we live. Therefore, we never know what might happen from day to day. Life isn't like it used to be. An old saying stated that if you live life cautiously and treat your neighbor right, you will die at an old age. This saying is not true because the young are dying quicker than the old. Diseases are killing thousands every day. The young as well as the old are dying in the thousands. Therefore, we don't have time to waste by not being real.

Churches are fighting with other churches. Christians are fighting with other Christians. Religions are fighting with other religions. Yet, we are supposed to be serving the same God. Let's just be real. We can not allow our opinions to make a fact just to prove that we are right. We must respect others and their beliefs. Once we show respect, we will earn the respect from others, all because we are real.

It is time to walk this walk in holiness. It is time to speak that which God has told us to speak. It is time to do what God has called us to do. It is time to grow in God. It is time for us to establish a relationship with God, a real relationship. It is time to accept the call of God and stay in his will. It is time to make the right choices and own up to our mistakes. It is time to plant our feet in the foundation of God and not turn back. It is time to walk in faith and conquer our fears. It is time to be real. Just be real . . .

Written By:
Elder Charlie A. Connor 3rd

# Epilogue

Thank God for all of you that purchased and read this book. I pray this book has helped you to be real with yourself so you can be real with God and reap the blessings. Please tell a friend or loved one about "Just Be Real" and how it helped you. Look for more books by Charlie A. Connor III as God continues to lead and guide me to declare and decree that the devil is a LIAR! If you have any comments, questions or concerns about this book, or would like to learn more information about Connor Ministries, you can reach me by emailing me @ charlieconnor137@hotmail.com. Be Blessed.

Elder Charlie A. Connor III
Connor Ministries

Contact author Elder Charlie A. Connor III
or order more copies of this book at


TATE PUBLISHING, LLC

127 East Trade Center Terrace
Mustang, Oklahoma 73064

(888) 361 - 9473

Tate Publishing, LLC

www.tatepublishing.com